ed Books *showing the way*

OCAL STREET ATLAS

C000055404

MEDWAY
GILLINGHAM

CHATHAM · FRINDSBURY · HALLING · HIGH HALSTOW
HIGHAM · RAINHAM · ROCHESTER · STROOD

CONTENTS

very effort has been made to verify the accuracy of information in this book but the publishers cannot accept responsibility for expense or loss caused by an error or omission.

Information that will be of assistance to the user of the maps will be welcomed.

representation on these maps of a road, track or path is no evidence of the existence of a right of way.

eet plans prepared and published by Red Books (Estate Publications) Ltd, Bridewell House, Tenterden, The Publishers acknowledge the co-operation of the local authorities of towns represented in this atlas.

Ordnance Survey® This product includes mapping data licensed from Ordnance Survey® with the permission of the Controller of Her Majesty's Stationery Office.

Crown Copyright   ISBN 978-1-84192-367-3   All rights reserved
Red Books (Estate Publications) Ltd   005-18a/09-05   Licence Number 100019031

www.redbooks-maps.co.uk

2007

LEGEND

	Pedestrianized / Restricted Access
	Track
	Built Up Area
- - - -	Footpath
	Stream
	River
Lock	Canal
▬■▬	Railway / Station
●	Post Office
P P+	Car Park / Park & Ride
C	Public Convenience
+	Place of Worship
→	One-way Street
i	Tourist Information Centre
▲8 ▲8	Adjoining Pages
	Area Depicting Enlarged Centre
	Emergency Services
	Industrial Buildings
	Leisure Buildings
	Education Buildings
	Hotels etc.
	Retail Buildings
	General Buildings
	Woodland
	Orchard
	Recreational / Parkland
	Cemetery

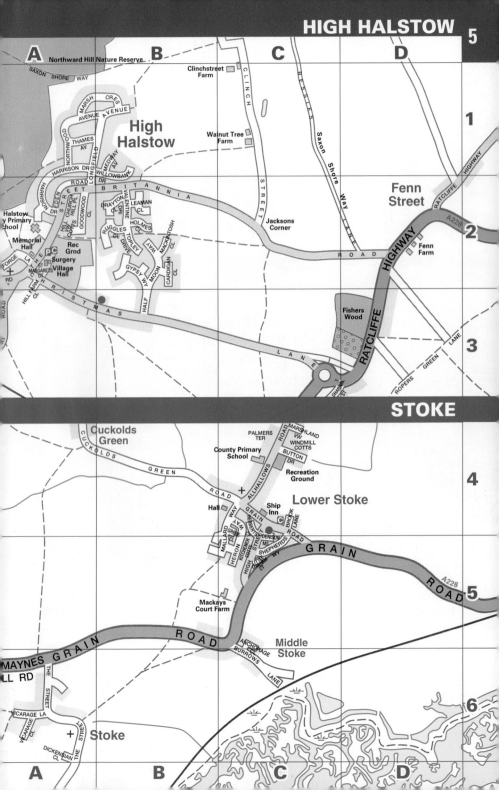

Cliffe Woods

Lower Higham

Lee Green

Mockbeggar

Reservoir

Little Oakleigh

Lillechurch Farm

Gore Green

White House Farm

Higham Memorial Hall

Higham County Primary School

Cliffe Woods County Primary School

Ratley Wood

Rec Grnd

Comm Centre

Reservoir

Dusty Hill

Sandy Hill

A B C D

1

Berry Court
Wood

Great
Chattenden
Wood

2

Lodge Hill
Camp

ROAD

LOCHAT

LODGE

DEPOT

Depot

Chattenden
Farm

HILL

Deangate Ridge
Municipal Golf Course

3

Ash
Wood

Round Top
Wood

Playing
Field

ELMWOOD RD

LODGE HILL LANE

SWINTON AV

RATCLIFFE

LOCHAT

4

CHATTENDEN
BARRACKS

CHILLIWACK

KIRBY

ROAD

Playing Field

Rams
Bottom
Wood

LINTORN
SIMMONDS RD

LANE

LINTORN
SIMMONDS
RD

ROAD

WAY

Chattenden

UPCHAT

ROAD

KITCHENER

OLD GEORGE RD

TUDOR

CHATTENDEN

A228

MAIN

HAIG
VILLAS

ROAD

Broad St

5

FIELD

School

School
HILL

OLD

ROAD

LANE

BALLS
COTTS

BROADWOOD

HOO
COMMON
RD

ELM

AVENUE

FOUR ELMS HILL

UPCHAT

BEACON HILL

HOO ROAD

ROAD

Playing
Field

6

ROAD

A289

B2108

ROAD

WAY

A228

Beacon Hill

Hoo
Common
Public Open
Space

Arethusa
Venture
Centre P

MARGETTS RD

Medway
Yacht Club

Saxon

Wilsonian
Sailing Club

BRISSENDEN
WAY

12

SCHOONER
WK

LEON
CUTTER

Lower
Upnor

A B C D

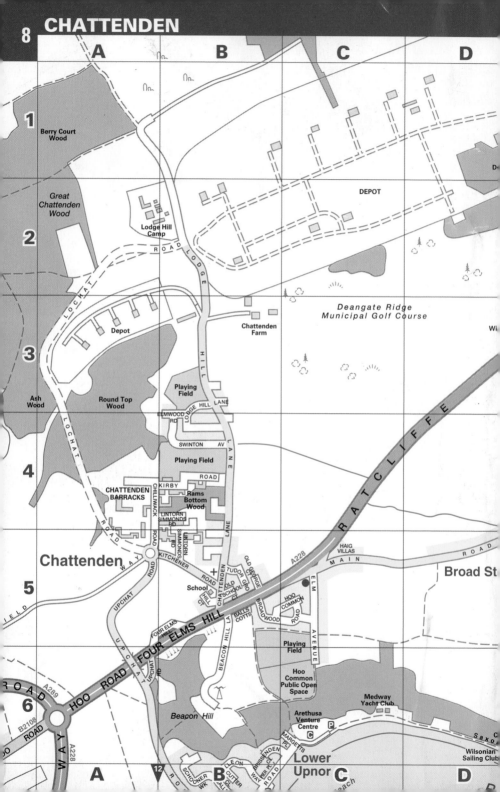

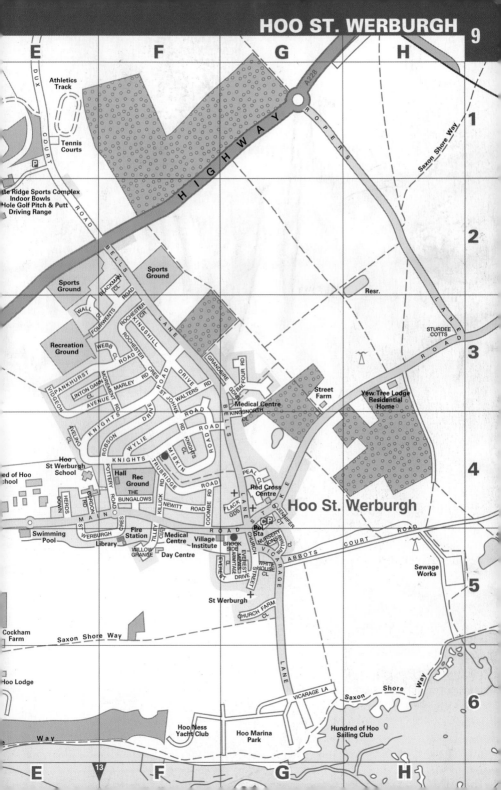

E   F   G   H

1

Athletics Track

Tennis Courts

P

DUX COURT

H I G H W A Y

A228

ROPERS

Saxon Shore Way

le Ridge Sports Complex
Indoor Bowls
Hole Golf Pitch & Putt
Driving Range

BELLS ROAD

2

Sports Ground

Sports Ground

Resr.

LANE ROAD

STURDEE COTTS

3

Recreation Ground

WALL CL

FOWRENTS

BLACKMAN CL

ROAD

ROCHESTER KNTCR

KINGSHILL

ROCHESTER CRES

LANE

GRANDSIRE

BALFOUR RD

Street Farm

Yew Tree Lodge Residential Home

WEBB

PANKHURST CL

UNTON DANN CL

MOREMENT RD

ROAD

AVENUE

MARLEY RD

ROCHESTER ROAD

ROAD

ST JOHNS ROAD

WALTERS RD

GEN

Medical Centre

KINGSNORTH

VIDGEON

KNIGHTS ROAD

AVELING CL

ROBSON RD

WYLIE DRIVE

MISKIN

DRIVE

KNIGHTS RD

ROAD

4

Hoo St Werburgh School

Hall

POTTERY ROAD

THE BUNGALOWS

Rec Ground

KNIGHTS

TRUBRIDGE RD

KILLICK

NEWITT ROAD

COOMBE ROAD

PEAL ROAD

Red Cross Centre

FLACK GDNS

LANE

ed of Hoo chool

HERDS DOWN

GORDON RD

MAIN ST WERBURGH

CRES

TILLEY

Fire Station

Medical Centre

BELLS

Pol Sta

CP

JENNIFER

ROAD

Hoo St. Werburgh

Swimming Pool

Library

WILLOW GRANGE

Day Centre

Village Institute

BROOK SIDE

ST WERBURGH

EVEREST DRIVE

EVEREST MEWS

HERMITAGE

CHURCH STREET

WHITE HOUSE CL

VICARAGE

ST JOHNS

WHITBREAD

ABBOTS COURT ROAD

Sewage Works

5

St Werburgh

CHURCH FARM CL

Cockham Farm

Saxon Shore Way

LANE

Hoo Lodge

VICARAGE LA

Saxon Shore Way

6

W a y

Hoo Ness Yacht Club

Hoo Marina Park

Hundred of Hoo Sailing Club

E   F   G   H

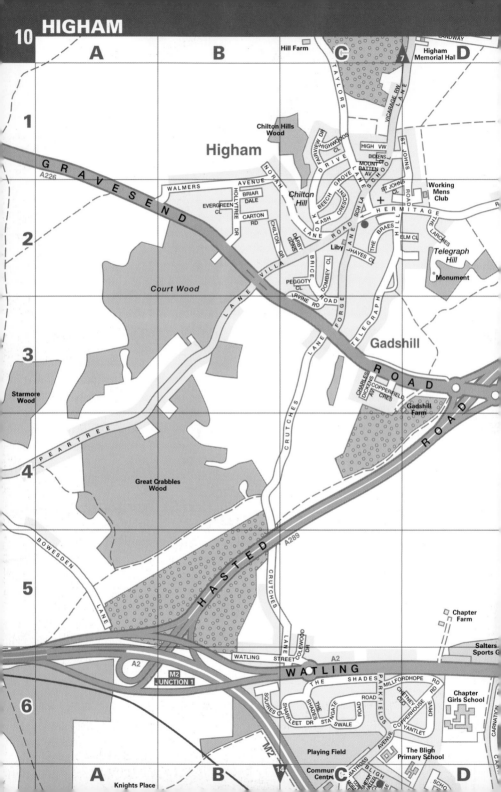

HIGHAM

Higham

Chilton Hills Wood

Hill Farm

Chilton Hill

Court Wood

Gadshill

Starmore Wood

Great Crabbles Wood

Telegraph Hill

Monument

Gadshill Farm

Chapter Farm

Salters Sports G

Chapter Girls School

The Bligh Primary School

Chapter Girls School

Playing Field

Communi Centre

Knights Place

GRAVESEND

A226

PEARTREE

BOWESDEN LANE

HASTED

A289

WATLING STREET

WATLING

A2

M2 JUNCTION 1

CRUTCHES LANE

VILLA LANE

FORGE LANE

TELEGRAPH

ROAD

ROAD

Higham Memorial Hall

LANDWAY

Working Mens Club

TAYLORS

VICARAGE RW LANE

ST JOHNS

HERMITAGE

THE LARCHES

ELM CL

THE BRAES

HILL

WALMERS AVENUE

EVERGREEN CL

BRIAR DALE

CARTON RD

HOLLYTREE DR

CHILTON DR

NORAH

BEECH GROVE

ASH LANE

HIGHWOODS

FAIRVIEW DR

DRIVE

DICKENS CL

HIGH VW

MOUNT BATTEN AV

SCH LA

CRESC

ROAD

Liby

HAYES CL

DOMBEY CL

DARBY GDNS

BRICE

PEGGOTY CL

IRVINE RD

CHARLES DICKENS AV

COPPERFIELD CRES

ROAD

THE SHADES

THE STANGATE

SHARFLEET DR

SQUIRES CL

COLEWOOD

CRUTCHES LANE

MILLFORDHOPE RD

CHENEY CL

COPPERHOUSE DRIVE

YANTLET AVENUE

PARKFIELDS

SWALE ROAD

BLIGH

BATROSS CL

CARNATION

SCHO

SWALE

A B C D

Chattenden

1

Noke Street

School

Four Elms Hill

Beacon Hill

2

HASTED

HOO ROAD

A289

B2108

A228

ROAD

Wainscott School

Cricket Ground

Frindsbury Tennis Club

Hall

UPNOR

HOLLYWOOD LANE

Memorial Hall

Rec Grnd

WAINSCOTT WK

3

Royal School of Military Engineering

Upnor Castle

WULFERE

WAINSCOTT ROAD

GILL AVENUE

UPNOR ROAD

TOWER HILL

HIGH ST

Wainscott

The Sanspareil PH

Hilltop School

Hilltop

4

BERWICK WAY

FRINDSBURY HILL

Sewage Works

Upper Upnor

ADMIRALTY RD

Tower Hill

Saxon Shore Way

Gundulph Pool

CASTLE STREET

VANGUARD WAY

MEDWAY TU

5

FRINDSBURY RD

Cemy

Rec Grnd

Sports Ground

LOALAND BUSINESS CENTRE

Maritime

NORTHPOINT BUSINESS EST

MEDWAY ENTERPRISE CENTRE

SPECTRUM BUSINESS ESTATE

MEDWAY CITY ESTATE

Whitewall Creek

Boat Slip Wharf

Euro Wharf

The Historic Dockyards

STATION

SHAMEL BUSINESS CENTRE

PHOENIX IND EST

WHITEWALL ROAD

ARDEN BUSINESS PARK

ROYAL EAGLE CL

6

STROOD

WESTFIELD BSNS CENTRE

Strood Pier

FINE LINE IND EST

Strood Reach

Gashouse Point

Crown Wharf

VICTORY BUSINESS PARK

Centre Court

CENTRAL BUSINESS PARK

NEPTUNE BUSINESS ESTATE

Thunderbolt Pier

A B 16 C D

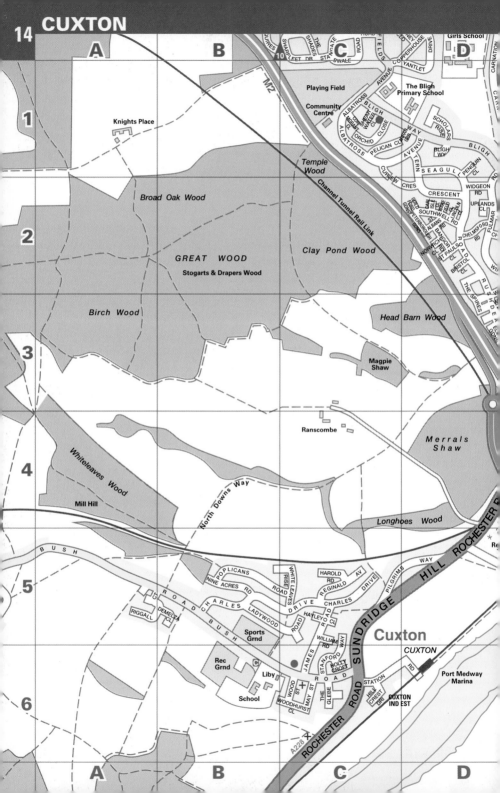

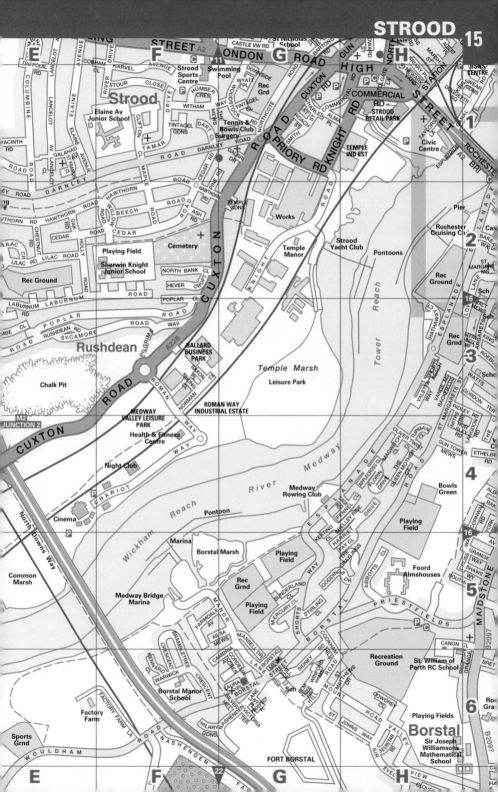

Strood

Rushdean

Borstal

FORT BORSTAL

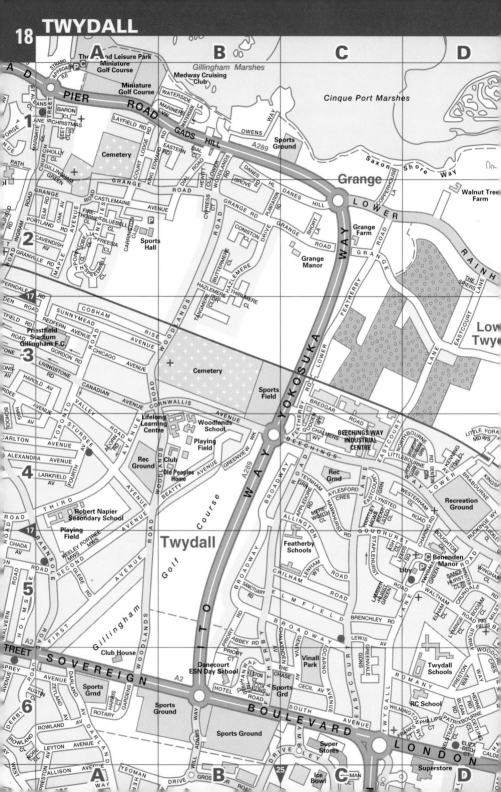

E   **F**   **G**   **H**

Ferol Peak

perhouse arshes

Horrid Hill

Rainham Creek

1

2

20

3

ourt ows try k

Sharpes Green

Riverside Country Park

Visitor Centre

ROAD

Manor Farm

nor urt

COWSTEAD LA

BLOORS WHARF RD

Bloors Wharf

Saxon Shore Way

LANE

LOWER

RAINHAM

WEST MOTNEY WY

MOTNEY

HILL ROAD

4

20

B2004

ROAD

5

Lower Rainham

BLOORS LANE

LOWER LANE

Berengrave Lane Nature Reserve

BERENGRAVE LANE

ROAD

RIVER VW

PUMP LANE

WOTTON CL
GREATLING CL
THORNHAM RB
EASTLING CL

WENDEN RB
CHINGS
BEECHINGS
BET GRN

Thames View Infants & Junior Schools

LICHFIELD
HEREFORD
TRURO
RIPON CL

MOT MOTH
CL
ELY CL

CHRIST FIELD
PEMBURY
PEMBURY
MELVILLE
PEMBURY WY

MACKLANDS WY

COBDOWN
GRO

LANDBOURNE PL

ELLISON WAY

WIVEN VIEW CL
COBDEN
TWYFORD
FINWELL

Eastcourt

Rainham Mark Grammar School

Playing Field

AVENUE

CLOSE
MORFOLK
DORSET SQ

PENSHURST CL

THE WILLOWS

HIGH ELMS

HOAKS

CRICKET Ground

LANE

CHALKY RD
ROYSTONS CL
IVEN GA
CL

WOOLERS CL

CHILDS CROFT
CROOM CROFT
DIGNALS
PKFIELD

BUSHMEADOW RD

BANK ROAD

ROBSON MEWS

STATION

WILLIAM STREET

TILBURY
FINWELL
ROAD

6

ANGDALE
BENSON
BEDFORD AV
STANFORD
CRANEORD

WAY
WAYS

Splashes Leisure Park

Cozenton Park

COZENTON CL

NORTHUMBERLAND

TUFTON RD

DEVON CL

RAINHAM

GRANARY CL
CAPER

WAKELEY RD

HENRY STREET

LINGHAM
SAXON

E   **F**   **G**   **H**

A B C D

Bartlett Creek

1

Bayford

2

Motney Hill

Sewage Works

19

MOTNEY HILL ROAD

Saxon Shore Way

3

Otterham Creek

Wharf

Horsham Marsh

Saxon Shore Way

Upchurch

Horsham Farm

HORSHAM HILL

HORSHAM LANE

Hall

ROAD

WOODRUFF CL

CROSIER CT

THE CH

4

CHAFFES TER

19

Wharf

Caravan Park

Mill Farm

LANE

SHADSHAW CL

BISHOP LA

Rec Grnd

CHAFFES

DRAKES CL

5

B2004

LOWER RAINHAM ROAD

GILLS TER

Otterham Quay

HORSHAM ROAD

WALLBRIDGE LANE

MARSTAN CL

ROAD

GRENADIER DR

GRE. CL

WILKS CL

LITTLE RD

River Valley Golf Course

OAK

CHAFFES

Gore Farm

6

WIVEN HO CL

CLOVER LA

TEN.

SU. SHORPE

HOMEFIELD

KENT TER

ODDEN CL

FORD WY

FINN

SHOREFIELDS

ACRE ROAD

WOOLBROOK

BURRSTOCK WAY

THORNE

CANTERBURY LANE

Club House

LINGHAM

STREET

HANKS FIELDS

REDSON CL

WAKELEY RD

A B C D

27

E   F   G   H

Millfordhope
Saltings

Twinney Creek

1

am
een

2

tham
een

Twinney
Saltings

Twinney
Wharf

Halstow Creek

3

Saxon Shore Way

4

ywell
Primary
hool

CHURCH
PATH

HALSTOW LANE

Sports
Ground

Sports
Ground

HERON CT

CURLEW AV

LAPWING DRIVE

THE GREEN

STREET

BURNTWICK DR

CROUCH HILL

VICARAGE LANE

Lower
Halstow

5

HOLYWELL LANE

Holywell
Farm

LANDRAIL
RD

SCHOOL LA

Memorial
Hall

WESTMORELAND
DRIVE

CUMBERL
AND DR

SCHOOL LANE

WARDWELL LANE

Home Farm

WESTFIELD
COTTS

Primary
School

6

HOLYWELL LANE

BREACH LANE

The
Laurels

E   F   G   H

BOXTED L

A B C D

1

2

3

4

5

6

School

FACTORY FARM LA

Silver
Victoria

Hilary
GDNS

NASHENDEN
ROAD
BURHAM ROAD
North Downs Way

FORT BORSTAL

Nashenden Farm

NASHENDEN FARM LANE

Channel Tunnel Rail Link

Shoulder of Mutton Wood

MEDWAY BRIDGE

St JOHNS WAY

SIR EVELYN ROAD
SECRETAN RD
VALLEY VIEW ROAD
COWDREY CL

Borstal

Rochester Girls Grammar School

Playing Fields

Sir Joseph Williamsons Mathematical School

CLOUDESLEY CL
TREVALE RD
TREVALE RD

B2097

COMPASS CL
HAWSER RD

THE SPINNAKER
WINDWARD CRE
FAI
ANCH

H.M. YOUTH CUSTODY CENTRE

Sports Grnd

SIR EVELYN ROAD

Playing Field

Res

HORWOOD CL

H.M. PRISON COOKHAM WOOD

SYLE WOOD CL
MONKWOOD RD
BARNWOOD CL

MAIDSTONE ROAD
WAKE RD
PILOT RD
KENT CL
BINNACLE

ARETHUSA

Playin Field

Thomas Aveling School

Playing Field

East Cookham Wood

COOKHAM WOOD

GALLEON CL

THE WARREN

LEANDER
ORION
EXETER
PENNANT

BRIDGEWOOD BUSINESS PK

MAIDSTONE ROAD

The Stirling Leisure Centre

Sports Fie

Nine Acre Wood

Little Monk Wood

Well Wood

Barn Wood

Gorse Wood

M2

LAKER

STONEY

ROCHESTER ROAD

AIRPORT INDUSTRIAL ES

Factories

LANKESTER PARKER RD

ROCHES AIRPO

Upper Nashenden Farm

HILL ROAD

Harris's Copse

Wouldham Common

MONK WOOD

Syle Wood

Channel Tunnel Rail Li

Middle Hill

A B C D

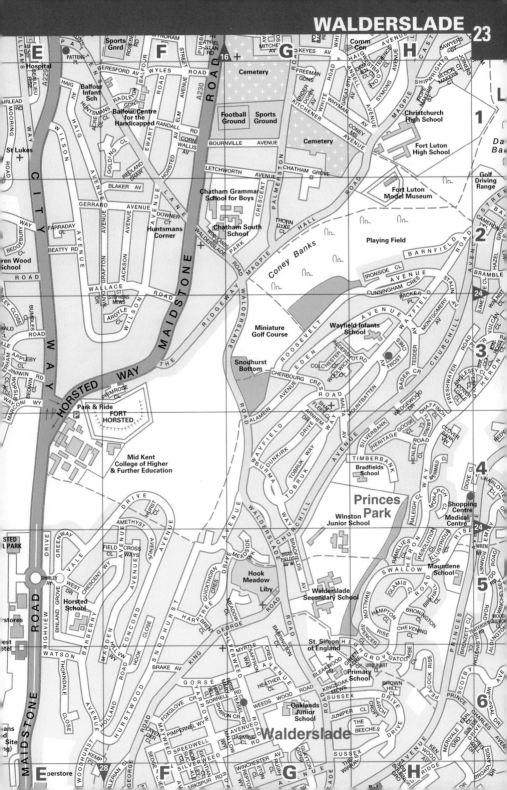

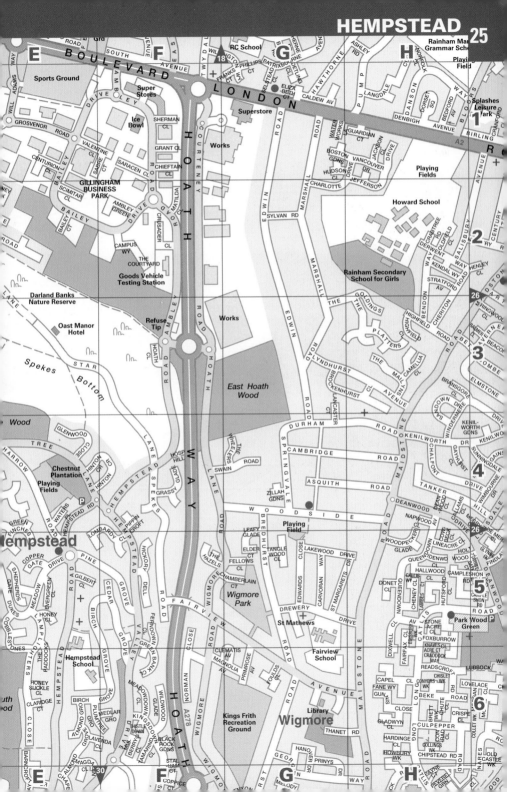

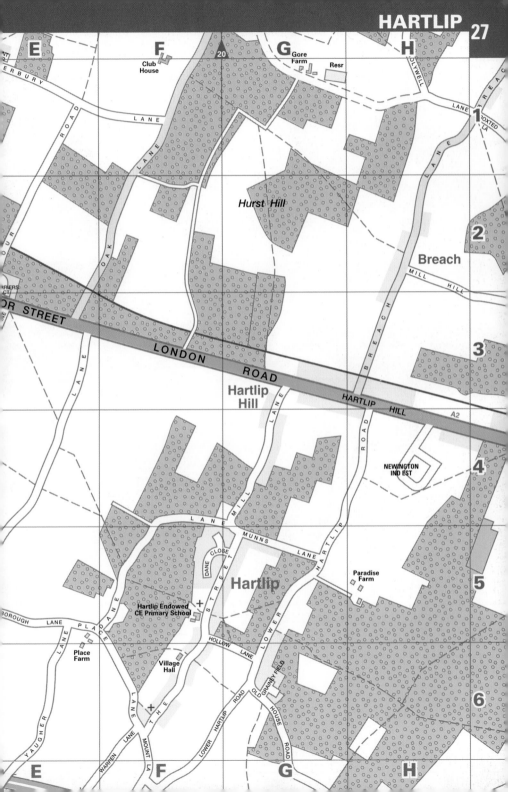

E
F
20
G Gore Farm
H
Club House
Resr

CANTERBURY
LANE
HOLYWELL
LANE
BREACH
OXTED LA
1

ROAD
OAK LANE
Hurst Hill
LANE
2
Breach

MILL HILL
RIERS CT
STREET
LONDON ROAD
BREACH
3

LANE
Hartlip Hill
MILL LANE
HARTLIP HILL
A2

ROAD
NEWINGTON IND EST
4

LANE
MUNNS LANE
HARTLIP ROAD
Paradise Farm
DANE CLOSE
STREET
5

BOROUGH LANE
PLACE LANE
DANE LANE
Hartlip
Hartlip Endowed CE Primary School
LOWER
HOLLOW LANE
Place Farm
Village Hall
OLD HOUSE ROAD
GRANNY FIELD
6

YAUGHER LANE
WARREN LANE
THE LANE
MOUNT LANE
LOWER HARTLIP ROAD

E
F
G
H

Syle Wood

Middle Hill

Bridges Wood

Middlehill Wood

B2097

Channel Tunnel Rail Link

Woolmans Wood Caravan Site (Touring)

Superstore

MAIDSTONE ROAD

CLOSE

HURST

HOLLAND AVENUE

B HURSTWOOD

COVE CR

ARROW

SORRELL

SHAW

TEASEL RD

WEEDS WOOD

D klands Junior School

Waldersl

CATKIN

MAYWEED

PIMPERNEL WY

MALLOW CL

JASMINE RD

AVENUE

SPEEDWELL

GENTIAN

SILVERWEED

WINCHESTER CL

GLATON CL

RUGBY

MANOR GDNS

KEMP CL

VALERIAN CL

CAMPION KING

NORTON GRO

GEORGE

CHESTNUT

SEDGE

ASPEN WY

LARKSPUR RD

REPTON WY

OAKHURST CL

OAK LAND CL

BULRUSH RD

WALDE

Bridgewood Manor Hotel

WALDERSLADE

HALLSFIELD

TADDINGTON WOODS

FARM

HILL

CHASE

YORK

AMANDA CL

MARSTON CL

WK

VICTORIA

OAKLEIGH

MONTFORD

AVENUE

AVENUE

NICKLAUS

MAFEKING

JACKLIN CL

TREVINO DR

LONG HURST DR

ROAD

TUNBURY

WALDERSLADE

ROBIN HOOD LANE

Swimming Pool

BUCKMORE PARK

Buckmore Park Activity Centre

Lord Lees

CHATHAM ROAD

CHATHAM ROAD

KEEFE CL

ROAD

TODDINGTON CRES

BARLING CLO

THORN CL

LAURIE GRAY AV

ROMAN CL

SADLERS CR

W TADDINGTON WOODS

PAPION GRO

HURST HILL

LOCKSLEY CL

LOWER ROBIN HOOD LANE

WAY

TUNBURY

OLLIFFES CL

FRIARS CL

SCHOOL HILL

LITTLE JOHN AV

BOLNER

FORESTERS CL

ROBIN HOOD LANE

Tunbury School

FERNBANK CL

FOSTINGTON

Rec Grnd

Hall

FRENSHAM WALK

MARLOW

HEPPLE WHITE

CHIPPENDALE

M2 JUNCTION 3

Hall

UPPER ROBIN HOOD M2

WOODBURY

FALKLAN

WALSHAM

SARSEN

ASHERATON

SHERATON

TAVI STOCK CL

CLOSE

AV STH

Blue Bell Hill

COMMON

CHATHAM ROAD

MAIDSTONE ROAD

MILL LANE

THE DOWNS

Picnic Site

Medway Crematorium

Impton Wood

WALDERSLADE

FALKLAND RD

ROAD

TUNBRYOAKS DENE

PODKIN WOODS

Podkin Wood

IMPTON

WOODS

FELDS

WARREN

Pits (Disused)

Kit's Coty

Kit's Coty Farm

SALISBURY ROAD

KINGSWOOD

CHATHAM ROAD

CHATHAM ROAD

Frith Wood

North Downs Wa

VINCENT RD

BERESFORD

RUSSELL RD

QUEENSWOOD

COLLINGWOOD RD

CHATHAM RD

OLD CHATHAM ROAD

A229

ROAD

Frith Wood

Westfie Wood

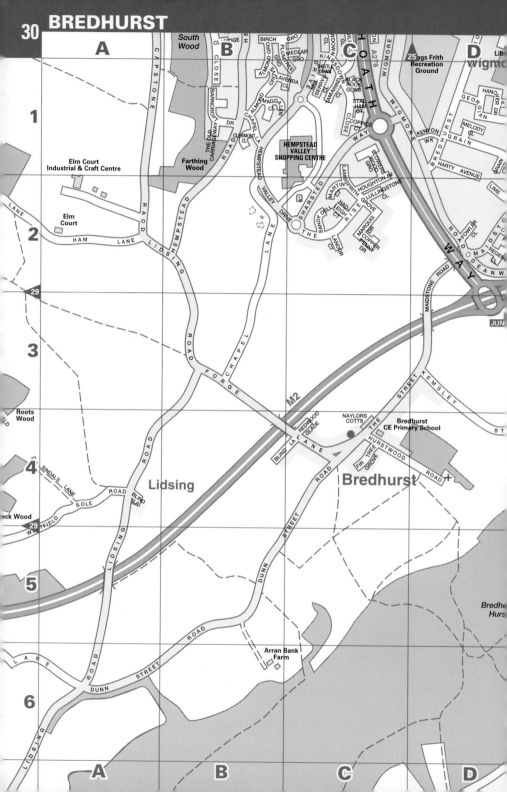

E **F** **G** **H**

BEKE ROAD
BRETT CL
CHUTE CL
CRISPE CL
GLADWYN CL
HARDINGE CL
HOWBURY WK
CULPEPPER
COW CL
COLLINGS WK
CHIPSTEAD RD
CLOSE
LONG
MORGA
COLLET WK
MOYLE CL
STYLE WK
CRAGIE CL
CANTERBURY
BAYSWATER
SANDGATE CT
HARCOURT
GREGORY CL
THRALE WAY
MIDDLETON CL
PEMBROKE GDNS
GDS
BULLINGTON GDNS
Park Wood

Medway Services

MERESBROUGH

26

M2

1

STIRLING CL
STANDEN CL
CLAVELL CL
SANDRINGHAM DRIVE
HUNSTANTON
BURNHAM WK
SOMERBY RD
SANDRINGHAM
BURNHAM WK

Dean Wood School

St Augustine of Canterbury R.C. Primary School

Yaugher Woods

HAWBECK ROAD
CATLIS ROAD
PLOMLEY ROAD
RYCAUT CL
ROWBROKE CL
PAYNE
D WALSINGHAM
WOLLASTON CL
CLOSE
HAWBECK ROAD
THORPE CL
SEDLEY CL
DRIVE
WILDMAN

Training & Conference Centre

Farthing Corner

ROAD

2

Breeches Broom Wood

Matts Hill Farm

HILL

Great Lennox Wood

3

ROAD
MATTS
WHITE
HILL

msley treet

Stone Acre Wood

Purple Hill

Yelsted

STREET MAGPIE LANE

LANE

ROAD

4

WHITE MAGPIE ROAD
ROAD
HILL
COX ROAD
YELSTED

LANE

ROAD

5

OAK
STREET
COX

Scragged Oak

RAGGED

YELSTED ROAD

6

E **F** **G** **H**

The Index includes some names for which there is insufficient space on the maps. These names are indicated by an * and are followed by the nearest adjoining thoroughfare.

Abbey Rd,
Frindsbury ME2 — 11 F5
Abbey Rd,
Twydall ME8 — 18 B5
Abbots Court Rd ME3 — 9 G5
Abbotts Cl ME1 — 15 H5
Abigail Cres ME5 — 28 D4
Abinger Dr ME5 — 29 G3
Absolam Ct ME8 — 18 D6
Academy Dr ME7 — 25 E1
Achilles Rd ME5 — 29 F3
Acorn Rd ME7 — 18 A4
Acre Cl ME4 — 23 E1
Adelaide Rd ME7 — 17 G4
Admirals Walk,
Lords Wood ME5 — 29 F1
Admirals Walk,
Rochester ME4 — 16 D1
Admiralty Rd ME2 — 12 D4
Admiralty Ter,
Brompton ME7 — 17 E1
Admiralty Ter,
Upper Upnor ME2 — 12 D4
Afghan Rd ME4 — 3 A3
Ailsa Mews ME1 — 15 F5
Aintree Rd ME5 — 29 G2
Airport
Ind Est ME1 — **22 D4**
Ajax Rd ME1 — 22 D3
Alamein Av ME5 — 23 G4
Albany Rd,
Chatham ME4 — 17 F6
Albany Rd,
Gillingham ME7 — 17 H4
Albany Rd,
Rochester ME1 — 16 A4
Albany Ter,
Chatham ME4 — 3 A3
Albany Ter,
Gillingham ME7 — 17 H3
Albatross Av ME2 — 14 C1
Albemarle Rd ME5 — 29 F3
Albert Pl ME2 — 11 H6
Albert Rd,
Chatham ME4 — 16 D5
Albert Rd,
Gillingham ME7 — 17 F4
Albert Rd,
Rochester ME1 — 16 A4
Albion Rd ME5 — 29 F3
Albury Cl ME5 — 29 G3
Aldershot Rd ME5 — 23 G3
Aldington Cl ME5 — 24 A6
Alexandra Av ME7 — 17 H4
Alexandra Glen ME5 — 29 F4
Alexandra Rd ME4 — 17 F6
Alfred Cl ME4 — 17 F6
All Saints Rd ME3 — 4 B3
Allen Cl ME5 — 24 A5
Allens Hill ME3 — 6 A1
Allhallows Rd ME3 — 5 C4
Allington Dr ME2 — 11 E5
Allington Rd ME8 — 18 C4
Allison Av ME7 — 24 D1
Alma Pl ME2 — 15 G1
Almon Pl ME1 — 3 C6
Almond Gro ME7 — 25 E6
Altbarn Ind
Centre ME5 — **29 G4**
Amanda Cl ME5 — 28 C1
Ambley Grn ME8 — 25 F2
Ambley Rd ME4 — 25 F3
Ambrose Hill ME5 — 17 G6
Amethyst Av ME5 — 23 F4
Amherst Hill ME7 — 16 D2
Amherst Rd ME1 — 16 B5
Amherst Redoubt
ME7 — 17 E2
Anchor Rd ME1 — 22 D1
Anchor Wharf ME4 — 16 D2
Anchorage Cl ME3 — 5 C5
Anglesey Cl ME5 — 23 H3
Ansell Av ME4 — 23 H1
Anson Cl ME5 — 24 A4
Anthonys Way ME2 — 12 B5
Apollo Way ME4 — 13 F3

Appleby Cl ME1 — 23 E3
Applecross Cl ME1 — 15 H4
Appledore Rd ME8 — 18 C4
Archer Rd ME5 — 24 A5
Archery Cl ME3 — 7 F2
Arden
Bsns Pk ME2 — **12 B6**
Arden St ME7 — 17 F2
Arethusa Rd ME1 — 22 D2
Argyle Cl ME1 — 23 F3
Armada Way ME4 — 16 D5
Armytage Cl ME3 — 9 G5
Arnhem Dr ME5 — 23 G4
Arnolde Cl ME2 — 16 C1
Arran Grn ME2 — 14 D1
Arthur Rd,
Rainham ME8 — 26 A2
Arthur Rd,
Rochester ME1 — 16 B5
Arundel Cl ME5 — 29 G3
Ascot Cl ME5 — 29 G3
Ash Cl, Luton ME5 — 24 B2
Ash Cl, Twydall ME8 — 18 C5
Ash Cres ME3 — 10 C2
Ash Rd ME2 — 15 F2
Ash Tree La ME5 — 24 C1
Ashby Cl ME2 — 6 C5
Ashcroft Rd ME3 — 12 A3
Ashenden Cl ME2 — 12 A4
Ashley Rd ME8 — 19 E6
Ashmead Cl ME5 — 29 F2
Ashwood Cl ME3 — 7 F2
Aspen Way ME5 — 28 C1
Asquith Rd ME8 — 25 G4
Association Walk
ME1 — 22 D3
Aston Cl ME5 — 29 E3
Athelstan Rd ME4 — 16 C6
Atlanta Ct ME4 — 16 B4
Audley Av ME7 — 24 D1
Austin Cl ME5 — 17 H6
Autumn Glade ME5 — 29 G4
Aveling Cl ME3 — 9 E4
Aveling Ct*,
North St ME2 — 11 H6
Avery Cl ME3 — 4 C2
Avery Way ME3 — 4 B3
Avocet Walk ME5 — 29 G3
Avondale Rd ME7 — 17 H2
Aylesford Cres ME8 — 18 C4

Backfields ME1 — 15 H3
Baden Rd ME7 — 17 H1
Bader Cres ME5 — 23 H3
Badger Rd ME5 — 29 F4
Baffin Cl ME4 — 16 D6
Bailey Cl ME8 — 25 E2
Bailey Dr ME5 — 25 E2
Bakenham Ho*,
The Fairway ME1 — 22 D1
Baker St ME1 — 16 A4
Bakers Walk ME1 — 3 B5
Balfour Rd,
Chatham ME4 — 16 C6
Balfour Rd, Hoo St
Werburgh ME3 — 9 G3
Ballard Bsns Pk
ME2 — **15 F3**
Ballard Ind
Centre ME5 — **29 G4**
Ballens Rd ME5 — 29 F1
Balls Cotts ME3 — 8 B5
Balmer Cl ME8 — 26 A3
Balmoral Rd ME7 — 17 G2
Bangor Rd ME2 — 14 D2
Bank St ME4 — 17 E5
Banks Rd ME2 — 11 H5
Bankside ME5 — 24 A2
Banky Fields Cl ME8 — 26 D1
Banning St ME7 — 17 H5
Barberry Av ME5 — 23 E6
Bardell Ter ME1 — 3 D6
Barfleur Manor*,
Middle St ME7 — 17 E1
Barkis Cl ME3 — 23 E3
Barleycorn Dr ME8 — 26 A4
Barleymow Cl ME5 — 24 A4
Barling Cl ME5 — 28 A4
Barlow Cl ME8 — 26 A6
Barnaby Ter ME1 — 16 A6
Barnard Ct ME4 — 16 D6
Barncroft Dr ME7 — 30 B1
Barnfield ME5 — 23 H2
Barnsole Rd ME7 — 17 H3

Barnwood Cl ME1 — 22 C2
Baron Cl ME7 — 18 A1
Barrier Rd ME4 — 16 D3
Barrington Cl ME5 — 23 G5
Barrowfield ME5 — 29 H3
Bartlett Cl ME5 — 29 G4
Barton Rd ME2 — 11 G6
Basi Cl ME2 — 12 A5
Batchelor St ME4 — 3 C2
Bath Hard La ME1 — 16 B3
Battlesmere Rd ME3 — 7 F1
Bayswater Dr ME8 — 26 A6
Beacon Cl ME8 — 26 A3
Beacon Hill ME5 — 17 G6
Beacon Hill La ME3 — 8 B6
Beacon Rd ME7 — 17 F5
Beaconsfield Av ME7 — 17 H3
Beaconsfield Rd ME4 — 16 D5
Bearsted Cl ME8 — 18 C4
Beatty Av ME7 — 18 B4
Beatty Rd ME1 — 23 E2
Beaufort Ct ME2 — 16 C2
Beaufort Rd ME2 — 11 E5
Beaulieu Rise ME1 — 16 B6
Bedford Av ME8 — 25 H1
Bedgebury Cl ME1 — 23 E2
Bedson Walk ME8 — 26 D1
Bedwin Cl ME1 — 23 E3
Beech Gro ME3 — 10 C2
Beech Rd ME2 — 15 F2
Beechen Bank Rd
ME5 — 29 E3
Beeching Rd ME5 — 29 F1
Beechings Grn ME8 — 19 E5
Beechings Way ME8 — 18 B4
Beechings Way
Ind Centre ME8 — **18 C3**
Beechmore Dr ME5 — 29 E3
Beechwood Av ME5 — 17 H6
Begonia Av ME8 — 18 D5
Beke Rd ME8 — 25 H6
Bell La ME14 — 29 E6
Bellgrove Ct ME5 — 29 E4
Bells La ME3 — 9 F2
Belmont Rd ME7 — 17 F3
Bendon Way ME8 — 25 H3
Benedict Cl ME2 — 6 D5
Benenden Rd ME2 — 12 A4
Bentley Cl ME5 — 29 F3
Berber Rd ME2 — 11 H5
Berengrave La ME8 — 19 G5
Beresford Av ME1 — 16 C6
Beresford Rd,
Gillingham ME7 — 17 H3
Beresford Rd,
Kit's Coty ME20 — 28 A6
Bergland Pk ME2 — 12 B5
Berkeley Cl ME1 — 23 E2
Berkshire Cl ME5 — 24 B3
Berwick Way ME2 — 12 B4
Bessies La ME3 — 5 C1
Best St ME4 — 3 B2
Bettescombe Rd ME8 — 26 A3
Beverley Cl ME8 — 26 B2
Bill Street Rd ME2 — 12 A4
Bilsington Cl ME5 — 24 A5
Bingham Rd ME2 — 12 A4
Bingley Rd ME1 — 16 B3
Binland Gro ME5 — 23 E5
Binnacle Rd ME1 — 22 D2
Binney Rd ME3 — 4 B3
Birch Dr ME5 — 29 H4
Birch Gro ME7 — 25 E6
Birchfields ME5 — 29 E2
Birkhall Cl ME5 — 23 H5
Birling Av ME8 — 25 H3
Bishop La ME9 — 20 D5
Bishops Walk ME1 — 3 C6
Bishopsbourne Grn
ME8 — 26 C2
Bittern Way ME4 — 13 G3
Black Rock Gdns ME7 — 25 F6
Blackman Cl ME3 — 9 F3
Blackthorn Av ME6 — 29 E2
Blackthorne Rd ME8 — 26 D2
Blaker Av ME1 — 23 F2
Bleakwood Rd ME5 — 23 G6
Blean Rd ME8 — 18 D6
Blenheim Av ME4 — 16 B6
Bligh Way ME2 — 14 C1
Blind La ME7 — 30 D6
Blockmakers Ct ME4 — 17 E6
Bloors La ME8 — 25 H1

Bloors Wharf Rd
ME8 — 19 G4
Blowers Wood Gro
ME7 — 30 C1
Blue Boar La ME1 — 3 C5
Bluebell Cl ME7 — 18 A2
Bodiam Cl ME8 — 18 D5
Bogarde Dr ME3 — 11 H3
Boley Hill ME1 — 3 B5
Bolner Cl ME5 — 28 D3
Bond Rd ME8 — 26 A6
Bonnington Grn ME8 — 19 E5
Booth Rd ME4 — 16 D5
Bootham Cl ME2 — 15 E3
Borough Rd ME7 — 17 G4
Borstal Mews ME1 — 15 G6
Borstal Rd ME1 — 15 H5
Borstal St ME1 — 15 G6
Boston Gdns ME8 — 25 G1
Boston Rd ME5 — 29 F3
Boughton Cl ME8 — 18 D5
Boundary Rd ME4 — 3 A3
Bournville Av ME4 — 23 F1
Bower Grn ME5 — 29 F4
Bowes Rd ME2 — 11 H6
Bowesden La ME3 — 10 A5
Bowman Cl ME5 — 23 F5
Boxley Cl ME5 — 29 F4
Boxley Rd ME5 — 29 E2
Brabourne Av ME8 — 18 D4
Bracken Hill ME5 — 29 E4
Bracken Lea ME5 — 24 A1
Brackwood Cl ME8 — 26 A5
Bradfields Av ME5 — 23 G5
Bradfields Av West
ME5 — 23 G5
Bradfords Cl ME4 — 13 F3
Bradley Rd ME2 — 6 A5
Bradshaw Cl ME9 — 20 D5
Brake Av ME5 — 23 F6
Brambledown ME5 — 24 A2
Brambletree Cres
ME1 — 15 F5
Bramley Cl ME8 — 26 D2
Bramley Rise ME2 — 11 E5
Bransgore Cl ME8 — 25 H3
Brasenose Rd ME7 — 17 H4
Brasted Ct ME2 — 11 G4
Breach La ME9 — 27 H3
Bredgar Rd ME8 — 18 C3
Bredhurst Rd ME8 — 25 G4
Brenchley Cl ME1 — 16 B6
Brenchley Rd ME8 — 18 C5
Brendon Av ME5 — 29 E1
Brent Cl ME5 — 23 F5
Brenzett Cl ME5 — 23 H6
Breton Rd ME1 — 16 A6
Brett Walk ME8 — 25 H6
Brewer Rd ME3 — 7 F2
Briar Dale ME3 — 10 B2
Brice Rd ME3 — 10 C2
Brick Field Vw ME2 — 12 A4
Bridge Rd,
Gillingham ME7 — 13 G6
Bridge Rd,
Rochester ME1 — 16 A6
Bridgewood
Bsns Pk ME1 — **22 C3**
Brier Cl ME5 — 24 A2
Bright Rd ME4 — 17 F5
Brindle Way ME5 — 29 G3
Brisbane Rd ME4 — 17 E5
Brissenden Cl ME2 — 12 D2
Bristol Cl ME2 — 14 D2
Britannia Cl ME2 — 6 D6
Britannia Rd ME3 — 5 B2
Britton St ME7 — 17 F3
Broadlands Dr ME5 — 29 F1
Broadview Av ME8 — 26 A2
Broadway ME8 — 18 B5
Broadwood Rd ME3 — 8 B5
Brockbank Cl ME5 — 29 E4
Bromley Cl ME5 — 24 A6
Brompton Cl ME4 — 16 D1
Brompton Farm Rd
ME2 — 11 F5
Brompton Hill ME4 — 16 D2
Brompton La ME2 — 11 G5
Brompton Rd ME7 — 17 E1
Bronington Cl ME5 — 23 H5
Brook La ME3 — 5 C4
Brooklyn Pad ME7 — 17 G1
Brookmead Rd ME3 — 7 F2

Brookside ME3 — 9 **⬤**
Broom Hill Rd ME2 — 11 **⬤**
Broomcroft Rd ME8 — 19 **⬤**
Brown St ME8 — 26 **⬤**
Browndens Rd ME2 — 6 **⬤**
Brownelow Copse
ME5 — 29 **⬤**
Brownhill Cl ME5 — 23 **⬤**
Bryant Rd ME2 — 11 **⬤**
Bryant St ME4 — 3 **⬤**
Buckingham Rd ME7 — 17 **⬤**
Buckland Cl ME5 — 29 **⬤**
Buckland Rd ME3 — 7 **⬤**
Bull La, Higham ME3 — 7 **⬤**
Bull La, Rochester ME1 — 3 **⬤**
Bulldog Rd ME5 — 29 **⬤**
Buller Rd ME4 — 16 **⬤**
Bulrush Cl ME5 — 28 **⬤**
Bumbles Cl ME1 — 3 **⬤**
Bunters Hill Rd ME3 — 7 **⬤**
Burgess Rd ME2 — 11 **⬤**
Burham Rd ME2 — 22 **⬤**
Burleigh Cl ME2 — 11 **⬤**
Burlington Gdns
ME8 — 31 **⬤**
Burma Way ME5 — 23 **⬤**
Burmarsh Cl ME5 — 24 **⬤**
Burnham Walk ME8 — 31 **⬤**
Burns Rd ME7 — 17 **⬤**
Burnt House Cl ME2 — 12 **⬤**
Burnt Oak Ter ME7 — 17 **⬤**
Burntwick Dr ME9 — 21 **⬤**
Burritt Mews ME1 — 16 **⬤**
Burritt St ME1 — 16 **⬤**
Burrows La ME3 — 5 **⬤**
Burrstock Way ME8 — 22 **⬤**
Burton Cl ME3 — 12 **⬤**
Bush Rd ME2 — 14 **⬤**
Bushmeadow Rd
ME8 — 19 **⬤**
Butt Haw Cl ME3 — 9 **⬤**
Buttermere Cl ME7 — 18 **⬤**
Button Dr ME3 — 5 **⬤**
Buttway La ME3 — 6 **⬤**
Buxton Cl ME5 — 29 **⬤**
Byron Rd ME7 — 17 **⬤**
Bythorne Cl ME8 — 26 **⬤**

Cadnam Cl ME2 — 11 **⬤**
Cagney Cl ME2 — 12 **⬤**
Caldecote Cl ME8 — 20 **⬤**
Caldonian Ct ME8 — 26 **⬤**
Caldew Av ME8 — 18 **⬤**
Callams Cl ME8 — 25 **⬤**
Callis Way ME8 — 25 **⬤**
Calthorpe Mews ME2 — 11 **⬤**
Cambria Av ME1 — 15 **⬤**
Cambridge Rd,
Gillingham ME8 — 25 **⬤**
Cambridge Rd,
Rochester ME2 — 11 **⬤**
Cambridge Ter ME4 — 3 **⬤**
Camden Cl ME5 — 24 **⬤**
Camden Rd ME7 — 13 **⬤**
Camellia Cl ME8 — 25 **⬤**
Cameron Cl ME5 — 24 **⬤**
Campion Cl ME5 — 29 **⬤**
Campleshon Rd ME8 — 25 **⬤**
Campus Way ME8 — 25 **⬤**
Canadian Av ME7 — 18 **⬤**
Canal Rd ME2 — 15 **⬤**
Canon Cl ME1 — 15 **⬤**
Canterbury La ME8 — 20 **⬤**
Canterbury St ME7 — 17 **⬤**
Capel Cl ME8 — 25 **⬤**
Capstone Rd ME5 — 24 **⬤**
Cardens Rd ME3 — 7 **⬤**
Cardigan Cl ME3 — 5 **⬤**
Carisbrooke Rd ME2 — 11 **⬤**
Carlisle Cl ME2 — 14 **⬤**
Carlton Av ME7 — 17 **⬤**
Carlton Cres ME5 — 24 **⬤**
Carnation Rd ME2 — 10 **⬤**
Carpeaux Cl ME4 — 3 **⬤**
Carpenters Cl ME1 — 16 **⬤**
Carpinus Cl ME5 — 29 **⬤**
Carrington Cl ME7 — 18 **⬤**
Carton Cl ME1 — 16 **⬤**
Carton Rd ME3 — 10 **⬤**
Carvoran Way ME8 — 25 **⬤**
Castle Av ME1 — 16 **⬤**
Castle Hill ME1 — 3 **⬤**
Castle Rd ME4 — 17 **⬤**
Castle St ME2 — 12 **⬤**

stle View Mews
IE1 3 B4
stle View Rd ME2 11 G6
stle Vw
sns Centre ME1 3 C4
stlemaine Av ME7 18 A2
therine St ME1 16 B5
tkin Cl ME5 28 C4
tterick Rd ME5 29 G2
vendish Av ME7 17 H2
vendish Rd ME1 16 B5
versham Cl ME8 26 C1
zeneuve St ME1 16 A3
cil Av,
illingham ME8 18 C6
cil Av,
ochester ME2 11 H5
cil Rd ME1 16 A4
dar Gro ME7 25 F5
dar Rd ME2 15 E2
lestine Cl ME5 29 E4
metery Rd ME2 6 C5
ntral Av ME4 13 E6
ntral Bsns Pk
ME2 16 C1
ntral Par ME1 16 A6
ntral Park Gdns
ME4 16 B5
ntral Rd ME2 11 G6
ntral Walk ME4 13 F3
nturion Cl ME8 25 E1
ntury Rd ME8 26 A2
ada Av ME7 17 H5
affes La ME9 20 D6
affes Ter ME9 20 D5
affinch Cl ME5 23 H4
alfont Dr ME8 25 H4
algrove Mews ME2 6 C5
alk Pitt Hill ME4 16 D5
alkenden Av ME8 18 B5
alky Bank Rd ME8 19 G5
almers Way ME8 18 C4
amberlain Ct ME8 25 G5
amberlain Rd ME4 17 F5
ancery Rd ME3 6 C2
apel Ct ME3 4 C5
apel La,
illingham ME7 30 B1
apel La,
ochester ME2 6 A5
apel Rd ME3 4 C5
aplin Cl ME3 12 A2
apter Rd ME2 11 F6
aring Rd ME8 18 D5
ariot Way ME2 15 E4
arles Dickens Av
ME3 10 C3
arles Dr ME2 14 B5
arles St,
Chatham ME4 16 C4
arles St,
Rochester ME2 15 G1
arlotte Cl ME5 24 A4
arlotte Dr ME8 25 G2
art Pl ME8 30 D2
arter St,
Chatham ME4 16 D6
arter St,
Gillingham ME7 17 F1
artwell Cl ME2 11 H4
artwell Ct ME4 3 A2
atham Gro ME4 23 G1
atham Hill ME5 17 E4
atham Mews ME4 13 F4
atham Rd ME5,20 28 A4
atsworth Dr ME2 11 H4
atsworth Rd ME7 17 G1
attenden La ME3 8 B5
aucer Cl ME2 12 C6
aucer Rd ME7 17 G5
egwell Dr ME5 23 H6
elmar Rd ME4 17 E4
elmsford Rd ME2 14 D2
eney Cl ME8 25 H5
equers Cl ME5 29 E4
equers Ct ME2 11 G4
erbourg Cres ME5 23 G3
eriton Rd ME8 25 H3
erry Amber Cl ME8 26 B2
erry Tree Rd ME8 26 B2
esham Dr ME8 26 A4
ester Cl ME2 14 D2
ester Rd ME7 17 H5
esterfield Cl ME8 19 F6
esterton Rd ME3 6 B2
estnut Av ME5 28 C2
estnut Rd ME2 15 E2
estnut Ter ME5 29 G3
etney Cl ME2 10 C6
evening Cl ME5 23 H5
Chicago Av ME7 18 A3
Chichester Cl ME8 26 C2
Chickfield Gdns ME5 17 G6
Chieftain Cl ME8 25 F1
Childscroft Rd ME8 19 G6
Chilham Cl ME4 3 A3
Chilham Rd ME8 18 B5
Chillington Cl ME2 6 A5
Chilliwack Rd ME3 8 A4
Chilton Ct ME8 19 F6
Chilton Dr ME3 10 B2
Chippendale Cl ME5 28 D4
Chipstead Rd ME8 25 H6
Chislet Walk ME8 25 H6
Christchurch Ct*,
High St ME5 24 B1
Christie Cl ME5 24 A4
Christmas La ME3 5 A2
Christmas St ME7 18 A1
Christopher Rd ME4 17 E5
Church Cl ME3 6 B1
Church Farm Cl ME3 9 G5
Church Farm Rd ME9 20 D4
Church Grn ME2 12 A5
Church Hill ME5 17 G6
Church Hill Pl ME3 5 A2
Church La ME4 16 D1
Church Mews ME8 26 B2
Church Path,
Rochester ME2 11 H6
Church Path,
Sittingbourne ME9 21 G4
Church St,
Chatham ME4 3 C3
Church St, Cliffe ME3 6 B3
Church St,
Gillingham ME7 18 A1
Church St,
Higham ME3 7 A3
Church St,
Hoo St Werburgh
ME3 9 G5
Church St,
Rochester ME1 16 A4
Church Ter ME5 17 G6
Churchill Av ME5 23 G5
Churchlands*,
Palmerston Rd ME4 23 G1
Chute Cl ME8 25 H6
Cinnabar Cl ME5 29 E4
City Way ME1 16 B4
Clandon Rd ME5 29 G2
Claremont Way ME4 3 C3
Clarence Av ME1 16 A4
Clarence Rd ME4 17 F6
Clarendon Dr ME2 11 G5
Claridge Ct ME7 25 E6
Clavell Cl ME8 31 F1
Cleave Rd ME7 17 H5
Clematis Av ME8 25 F6
Clermont Cl ME7 30 B1
Cleveland Rd ME7 17 H1
Cliffe Ct ME3 6 B1
Cliffe Rd ME2 11 G4
Clifton Cl ME2 15 F1
Clifton Rd ME7 17 G1
Clinch St ME3 5 C1
Clinton Av ME2 11 E5
Clipper Cl ME2 16 C1
Clipper Ct ME2 16 C1
Clive Rd ME1 16 A4
Cloisterham Rd ME1 23 E3
Cloudesley Cl ME1 22 C1
Clover Bank Vw ME5 23 H4
Clover Lay ME8 20 A6
Clover St ME4 3 B3
Coachmans Mews
ME1 3 C6
Coast Guard Cotts
ME3 4 C6
Cobb Cl ME2 11 E5
Cobden Rd ME4 17 F5
Cobdown Gro ME8 19 H5
Cobham Cl ME2 11 E6
Cobham Rise ME7 18 A3
Coblestones ME7 25 E5
Cobtree Cl ME5 24 A2
Colchester Cl ME5 23 G3
Colewood Dr ME2 10 C6
College Av ME7 17 F3
College Rd ME4 13 E6
College Yd ME1 3 B5
Collet Walk ME8 26 A6
Collings Walk ME8 25 H6
Collingwood Rd
ME20 28 A6
Collis St ME2 11 G5
Columbine Cl ME2 11 E6
Columbine Rd ME2 15 E1
Commercial Rd ME2 15 H1
Commissioners Rd
ME2 12 A5
Common La ME3 6 C1
Common Rd,
Chatham ME5 28 A4
Common Rd,
Rochester ME3 7 F4
Common Wall ME3 6 D1
Compass Cl ME1 22 D1
Compton Cl ME5 29 H3
Concord Av ME5 23 F5
Coney Mews ME4 23 H1
Conifer Dr ME5 29 G4
Coniston Cl ME7 18 B2
Connaught Rd,
Chatham ME4 17 F6
Connaught Rd,
Gillingham ME7 17 G3
Conrad Cl ME8 25 H6
Constitution Hill ME5 17 F5
Constitution Rd ME5 17 F5
Conway Cl ME2 11 E5
Conway Mews ME7 17 E2
Conyers Walk ME8 25 H6
Cooden Cl ME8 19 H6
Cook Cl ME5 24 A4
Cookham Hill ME1 15 G5
Cookham Wood Rd
ME1 22 C3
Cooling Rd, Cliffe ME3 6 B3
Cooling Rd,
High Halstow ME3 5 A2
Cooling Rd,
Rochester ME2 11 H3
Cooling St ME3 6 D3
Coombe Cl ME5 29 F1
Coombe Rd ME3 9 F4
Cooper Rd ME5 29 E2
Copenhagen Rd ME7 17 G3
Copperfield Cres ME3 10 C3
Copperfield Rd ME1 16 A6
Coppergate ME7 25 E5
Copperhouse La ME7 18 C2
Copperhouse Rd ME2 10 C6
Copperpenny Dr ME7 30 C2
Coppice Ct ME7 30 C1
Coppice Rd ME5 29 F2
Cordelia Cres ME1 15 G6
Corkwell St ME4 16 C5
Cormorant Apprts
ME4 13 F4
Cormorant Cl ME2 14 C1
Cornwall Rd,
Gillingham ME7 17 G1
Cornwall Rd,
Rochester ME1 16 A4
Cornwallis Av,
Chatham ME4 23 F1
Cornwallis Av,
Gillingham ME7 18 B3
Coronation Rd,
Chatham ME5 17 G6
Coronation Rd,
Rochester ME3 4 C5
Corporation Rd ME7 17 H1
Corporation St ME1 3 B4
Corral Cl ME5 17 H6
Corys Rd ME1 16 A2
Cossack St ME1 16 A4
Cossington Rd ME5 29 E4
Cottage Rd ME4 16 D2
Cottall Av ME4 16 D6
Coulman St ME7 17 H3
Court Lodge Rd ME7 18 A1
Courteney Rd ME8 25 F1
Courtfield Av ME5 29 F3
Coventry Cl ME2 15 E2
Coverdale Cl ME5 23 H3
Cowbeck Cl ME8 25 H5
Cowdrey Cl ME1 15 H6
Cowper Rd ME7 17 G5
Cowstead La ME8 19 F4
Cox Gdns ME8 18 B6
Cox St ME14 31 F6
Cozenton Cl ME8 26 A1
Crabtree Rd ME8 25 H2
Craddock Way ME8 25 H6
Cragie Walk ME8 26 A6
Cranbrook Cl ME8 18 D5
Cranford Cl ME8 26 A1
Cranleigh Gdns ME4 16 B5
Cranmere Ct ME2 12 A5
Crescent Way ME5 23 E5
Cressey Ct ME4 3 A3
Crest Rd ME1 16 A6
Crestway ME5 24 A2
Crispe Cl ME8 25 H6
Crispin Rd ME2 11 E5
Croft Cl ME5 29 G4
Cromer Rd ME2 11 H5
Cromwell Ter ME4 17 E5
Crosier Ct ME9 20 D4
Crosley Rd ME7 17 H5
Cross St,
Chatham ME4 3 C2
Cross St,
Gillingham ME7 17 G2
Cross St,
Rochester ME2 11 H5
Cross Ways ME1 16 A5
Crossways ME5 23 F5
Crouch Hill Ct ME9 21 G5
Crow La ME1 3 C6
Crown St ME7 17 G2
Croydon Cl ME5 29 F1
Crundale Rd ME8 18 D5
Crusader Cl ME8 25 F2
Crutches La ME2 10 B5
Cuckolds Green Rd
ME3 5 A4
Culpeper Cl ME2 16 B1
Culpepper ME8 25 H6
Culpepper Rd ME8 31 E1
Cumberland Dr ME9 21 G5
Cumberland Rd ME7 13 F6
Cunningham Cres
ME5 23 H3
Curlew Av ME9 21 G5
Curlew Cres ME2 14 C1
Curtis Way ME1 23 E3
Curzon Rd ME4 16 D5
Cutter Cl ME2 12 D2
Cuxton
Ind Est ME2 14 C6
Cuxton Rd ME2 15 E4
Cygnet Rd ME5 29 F3
Cypress Ct ME7 18 B2
Cypress Rd ME2 12 A4

Daffodil Rd ME2 11 E6
Dagmar Rd ME4 17 E6
Dale Ct ME5 29 E3
Dale Rd ME1 16 A5
Dale St ME4 16 C6
Dalison Ct ME2 6 D6
Dalton St ME7 17 G2
Damien Cl ME4 17 E6
Dane Cl,
Chatham ME5 29 F3
Dane Cl,
Sittingbourne ME9 27 F5
Dane La ME9 27 F5
Danes Hill ME7 18 B1
Danson Way ME8 25 H1
Darby Gdns ME3 10 C2
Darenth Rise ME5 29 F2
Dargets Rd ME5 29 E1
Darland Av ME7 18 A6
Darnley Cl ME2 15 E1
Darnley Rd ME2 15 E2
Dart Cl ME2 15 F1
Darwin Ct ME1 16 B3
Dashmonden Cl ME2 12 A3
Davenport Av ME7 17 H1
Davy Ct ME1 3 C6
Dawes St ME7 17 F3
De Mere Cl ME8 26 A5
Deacon Cl ME2 11 F6
Dean Rd ME2 11 F6
Deanwood Cl ME8 25 H4
Deanwood Dr ME8 26 A5
Deering Cl ME4 13 F3
Defiant Cl ME5 24 A4
Defoe Cl ME5 24 A4
Delce Rd ME1 16 B3
Demelza Cl ME2 14 B5
Denbigh Av ME8 25 H1
Denison Mews ME3 5 C5
Denton Grn ME8 18 D4
Derby Rd ME5 17 H6
Derwent Way ME8 25 H2
Detling Cl ME8 18 D6
Devon Cl,
Chatham ME5 24 B3
Devon Cl,
Gillingham ME8 26 B1
Devonshire Rd ME7 17 G1
Dewberry Cl ME4 13 F4
Dial Cl ME7 18 B1
Dial Rd ME7 18 B2
Diana Rd ME4 17 E5
Dickens Ct,
Higham ME3 10 C1
Dickens Ct,
Rochester ME2 12 B6
Dickens Rd ME1 16 A5
Dickensian Cl ME3 5 A6
Dignals Cl ME8 19 G6
Dillywood Flds ME3 11 E4
Dillywood La ME3 11 E4
Dixwell Cl ME8 25 H6
Dock Rd ME4 16 D2
Doddington Rd ME8 19 E5
Doggetts Row ME3 4 C5
Doggetts Sq ME2 15 H1
Dogwood Cl ME5 29 H4
Dolphin Dr ME8 26 A6
Dombey Cl,
Higham ME3 10 C2
Dombey Cl,
Rochester ME1 16 A5
Donet Cl ME8 25 H5
Dongola Rd ME2 11 H5
Dorchester Cl ME3 7 E2
Dornden Gdns ME5 29 F2
Dorrit Way ME1 16 B6
Dorset Sq ME8 25 H1
Dotterel Cl ME5 29 G3
Doust Way ME1 16 B3
Dove Cl ME5 23 H4
Downer Ct ME1 23 F2
Downside ME2 11 G6
Downsview ME5 24 A2
Drakes Av ME2 11 G5
Drakes Cl ME9 20 D5
Drayton Cl ME3 5 B2
Drewery Dr ME8 25 G5
Duchess Cl ME2 11 E5
Duchess of Kent Dr
ME5 29 E2
Dukes Meadow Dr
ME7 25 E4
Duncan Rd ME7 17 G3
Dunkirk Dr ME5 23 G4
Dunlin Dr ME4 13 G3
Dunn Street Rd ME14 30 A6
Dunnings La ME1 16 A3
Durham Rd ME8 25 G4
Durling Ct ME8 26 D1
Durrell Gdns ME5 24 A1
Duval Dr ME1 23 F2
Dux Court Rd,
High Halstow ME3 5 A3
Dux Court Rd,
Hoo St Werburgh
ME3 9 E1

Ealing Cl ME5 24 A6
Earl Cl ME5 23 H6
East End Rd ME4 13 G5
East Hill ME5 24 B2
East Rd ME4 12 D6
East Row ME1 3 C6
East St,
Chatham ME4 17 E5
East St,
Gillingham ME7 17 G2
Eastcourt Grn ME8 18 C4
Eastcourt La ME7,8 18 C6
Eastern Rd ME7 18 B1
Eastgate ME1 3 C6
Eastgate Ct ME1 3 C6
Eastgate Ter ME1 3 C6
Eastling Cl ME8 19 E5
Eden Av ME5 23 G3
Eden Rd ME3 5 A2
Edgeway ME4 13 E3
Edinburgh Rd,
Chatham ME4 17 F6
Edinburgh Rd,
Gillingham ME7 17 G3
Edinburgh Rd,
Rochester ME3 4 C5
Edisbury Walk ME8 25 H5
Edward St,
Chatham ME4 17 E5
Edward St,
Rochester ME2 11 H6
Edwards Cl ME8 25 G5
Edwin Rd ME8 25 G3
Egret Cl ME4 13 E4
Elaine Av ME2 15 E1
Elder Ct ME8 25 G5
Eldon St ME4 3 D2
Elford Rd ME3 6 B2
Elgin Gdns ME2 14 D3
Elham Cl ME8 18 D5
Elizabeth Ct ME8 25 G1
Ellison Way ME8 19 H6
Elm Av,
Chatham ME4 23 F1
Elm Av,
Rochester ME3 8 C5
Elm Cl ME3 10 C2
Elm Rd ME7 18 A2
Elm Tree Dr ME1 15 G6
Elmfield ME8 18 B5
Elmhurst Gdns ME4 16 B5
Elmstone Rd ME8 26 A3
Elmwood Rd ME3 8 A4

Ely Cl ME8 19 F5
Embassy Cl ME7 24 D2
Emerald Cl ME1 23 E3
Emily Rd ME5 24 A5
Englefield Cres ME3 7 F2
Enterprise Cl ME2 12 B5
Ernest Rd ME4 17 E5
Esplanade ME1 3 A6
Essex Rd ME2 6 C4
Estelle Cl ME1 23 E3
Ethelbert Rd ME1 16 A4
Eton Cl ME5 28 D1
Eva Rd ME7 17 G5
Evelyn Cl ME2 12 A5
Everest Dr ME3 9 F5
Everest La ME2 11 H5
Everest Mews ME3 9 G5
Evergreen Cl,
Gillingham ME7 25 E6
Evergreen Cl,
Rochester ME3 10 B2
Ewart Rd ME4 23 F1
Exeter Walk ME1 22 D3
Exmouth Rd ME7 13 G6
Exton Cl ME5 29 F3

Factory Farm La ME1 15 F6
Fagus ME5 29 E4
Fairfax Cl ME8 25 H6
Fairlead Rd ME1 23 E1
Fairview Av ME8 25 F5
Fairview Dr ME3 10 C1
Fairway Cl ME1 22 D1
Falkland Pl ME1 28 C4
Fallowfield ME5 24 A2
Fanconi Rd ME5 29 F2
Fane Way ME8 25 H6
Farley Cl ME5 29 H2
Farm Hill Av ME2 11 F4
Farm Rd ME5 28 C2
Farmdale Av ME1 15 F5
Farnham Cl ME8 26 D2
Farraday Cl ME1 23 E2
Farriers Ct ME8 27 E2
Fay Cl ME1 15 H5
Featherby Rd ME8 18 B6
Feldspar Cl ME5 28 D4
Fellows Cl ME8 25 G5
Fennel Cl ME1 15 G4
Fernbank Cl ME5 28 C3
Ferndale Rd ME7 17 H2
Ferndown Cl ME7 25 F5
Ferrier Cl ME8 26 A6
Ferry Rd ME2 6 D5
Field Cl ME5 23 F5
Fieldworks Rd ME4 13 E6
Findlay Cl ME5 26 A5
Fine Line
  Ind Est ME2 12 B6
Finwell Rd ME8 19 H6
Fir Tree Gro ME5 29 G4
Firethorne Cl ME7 18 A2
First Av,
  Chatham ME4 17 G6
First Av,
  Gillingham ME7 18 A5
Firtree Gro ME4 30 C4
Fisher Rd ME3 23 H3
Five Bells La ME1 16 B3
Flack Gdns ME3 9 G4
Flamingo Cl ME5 23 H4
Flaxmans Ct ME7 17 E1
Fleet Rd ME1 23 E1
Flint Grn ME5 29 F2
Florence St ME2 11 H5
Florin Dr ME1 15 H4
Foord St ME1 16 A3
Fordwich Dr ME3 11 G3
Fordwich Grn ME8 18 D5
Forest Dr ME5 28 D3
Forestdale Rd ME5 29 E5
Foresters Cl ME5 28 D3
Forge La,
  Bredhurst ME7 30 B3
Forge La,
  Gillingham ME7 17 H1
Forge La,
  High Halstow ME3 5 A2
Forge La,
  Higham ME3 10 C3
Forge La,
  Sittingbourne ME9 20 D4
Formby Rd ME2 6 C4
Fort Pitt Hill ME1 3 A2
Fort Pitt St ME4 3 A3
Fort St ME1 16 B4
Fostington Way ME5 28 C4
Foulds Cl ME8 25 G6
Fountain Rd ME2 11 E5
Four Elms Hill ME3 8 A6

Fourth Av ME8 18 A4
Fourwents Rd ME3 9 E3
Fowey Cl ME5 24 A5
Fowler Cl ME8 30 D2
Fox St ME7 17 F2
Foxburrow Cl ME8 25 H5
Foxglove Cres ME5 23 F6
Foxtail Cl ME4 13 F4
Francis Dr ME5 29 E3
Franklin Rd ME7 17 G3
Franks Ct ME8 18 C6
Freasia Cl ME7 18 A2
Frederick Rd ME7 17 F4
Freeman Gdns ME4 16 D6
Frensham Walk ME5 28 D3
Freshwater Rd ME5 23 H3
Friars Av ME5 28 D3
Friary Pl ME2 11 H6
Frindsbury Hill ME2 12 A4
Frindsbury Rd ME2 11 H6
Frinsted Cl ME8 19 E5
Friston Way ME1 23 E2
Frittenden Rd ME8 12 B4
Frobisher Gdns ME1 16 A4
Frost Cres ME5 23 H3
Fry Cl ME3 4 C5
Fulmar Rd ME2 14 D2
Furrells Rd ME1 3 D6

Gads Hill ME7 18 B1
Gainsborough Cl
  ME8 26 A4
Galahad Av ME2 15 E1
Galbri Dr ME2 15 G1
Galena Cl ME5 29 E4
Galleon Cl ME1 22 D3
Galleon Way ME2 12 D2
Gardenia Cl ME2 11 H4
Gardiner St ME7 17 G2
Garfield Rd ME7 17 H1
Gas House Rd ME1 3 C4
Gatcombe Cl ME5 23 H6
Gate Rd ME4 13 G5
Gatekeeper Chase
  ME8 26 B2
Gayhurst Cl ME8 25 H4
Gean Cl ME5 29 E4
Geneva Av ME8 18 C5
Gentian Cl ME5 28 C1
George La ME1 3 B4
George Summers Cl
  ME2 12 C5
Georgian Way ME8 30 D1
Gerald Av ME4 16 D6
Gerrard Av ME1 23 E2
Gibraltar Av ME7 17 E1
Gibraltar Hill ME1 3 B3
Gifford Cl ME8 19 E4
Gilbert Cl ME7 25 E5
Gill Av ME2 12 B3
Gillingham
  Bsns Pk ME8 25 E2
Gillingham Grn ME7 18 A1
Gillingham Rd ME7 18 A1
Gills Cotts ME1 16 B3
Gills Cl ME2 12 B6
Gills Ter ME8 20 B5
Ginsbury Cl ME2 16 C2
Gladstone Rd ME4 16 C5
Gladwyn Cl ME8 25 H6
Glamford Rd ME2 15 E2
Glamis Cl ME5 23 H5
Glanville Rd,
  Gillingham ME7 17 H3
Glanville Rd,
  Rochester ME2 11 G6
Glayton Gdns ME5 28 D1
Gleaming Wood Dr
  ME5 29 G5
Gleanings Mews ME1 3 A6
Glebe Rd ME7 18 A5
Glencoe Rd ME4 16 D5
Glenwood Cl,
  Chatham ME4 24 B2
Glenwood Cl,
  Gillingham ME8 25 H1
Glistening Glade
  ME8 26 A4
Globe La ME4 3 B1
Gloucester Cl ME8 26 C2
Glovers Mill ME1 16 A4
Glynne Cl ME8 26 A5
Goad Av ME5 29 F1
Godden Way ME8 18 C4
Goddings Dr ME1 15 G5
Goddington Rd ME1 15 H5
Godfrey Cl ME7 11 F4
Goldcrest Dr ME4 13 F3
Golden Wood Cl ME5 29 G4
Golding Cl ME1 23 F1

Goldsmith Rd ME8 26 A6
Goldstone Walk ME5 29 E4
Goldsworth Dr ME2 11 G4
Goodall Cl ME8 26 A5
Goodwin Rd ME3 7 F2
Goodwood Cl ME3 5 A2
Goose Cl ME5 23 H4
Gordon Rd,
  Brompton ME7 17 E1
Gordon Rd,
  Chatham ME4 17 E6
Gordon Rd,
  Gillingham ME7 17 H3
Gordon Rd,
  Hoo St Werburgh
  ME3 9 E4
Gordon Rd,
  Rochester ME2 11 G6
Gordon Ter ME1 16 A3
Gore Green Rd ME3 7 A3
Gorse Av ME5 23 F6
Gorse Rd ME2 11 F5
Gorst St ME7 17 E1
Goudhurst Rd ME8 18 C5
Gould Rd ME5 29 E1
Grafton Av ME5 23 F2
Graham Cl ME7 16 D1
Grain Ct ME8 30 D1
Grain Rd,
  Gillingham ME8 30 D1
Grain Rd,
  Isle of Grain ME3 4 A6
Grain Rd, Stoke ME3 5 A6
Grainey Fld ME9 27 G6
Granary Cl ME8 26 B1
Grandsire Gdns ME3 9 F3
Grange Hill ME5 17 F5
Grange Rd,
  Gillingham ME7 18 A2
Grange Rd,
  Rochester ME2 11 H6
Grange Way ME1 16 A5
Grant Cl ME8 25 F1
Grant Rd ME3 12 A2
Granville Rd ME7 17 H2
Grasmere Gro ME2 12 A4
Grassy Glade ME7 25 F4
Gravel Walk ME1 16 A3
Graveney Cl ME3 7 F3
Gravesend Rd ME3 10 A1
Grayne Av ME3 4 C5
Great Lines ME7 17 E2
Great South Av ME4 23 G1
Grebe Cl ME3 5 C4
Green Bank Cl ME7 25 F5
Green Cl ME5 16 A6
Green La, Cliffe ME3 6 C1
Green La,
  Isle of Grain ME3 4 C5
Green St ME7 17 G2
Greenacre Cl ME5 23 G6
Greenbank ME5 24 A2
Greenfield Rd ME7 17 H2
Greenfields Cl ME3 12 B2
Greenfinches ME7 25 F4
Greensands ME5 29 F5
Greenvale Gdns ME8 18 C5
Greenview Walk ME7 18 B4
Greenway ME5 23 E5
Greenwich Cl ME3 24 A6
Gregory Cl ME8 26 A6
Grenadier Cl ME8 20 A6
Gresham Cl ME8 26 B1
Grizedale Cl ME1 23 E2
Grosvenor Av ME4 16 C5
Grosvenor Rd ME8 25 E1
Grove Rd,
  Chatham ME4 17 F6
Grove Rd,
  Gillingham ME7 18 B2
Grove Rd,
  Rochester ME2 11 H5
Grove Rd,
  Upper Halling ME2 6 A5
Guardian Ct ME8 25 H1
Guildford Gdns ME2 14 D2
Guinness Dr ME3 11 H3
Gun La ME7 11 H6
Gun Tower Mews
  ME1 15 H4
Gundulph Rd ME4 3 A2
Gundulph Sq ME1 3 B4
Gunnis Cl ME8 25 H6
Gypsy Way ME3 5 B2

Hadleigh Ct ME8 30 C2
Haig Av,
  Chatham ME4 17 E6
Haig Av,
  Gillingham ME7 17 H3

Haig Av,
  Rochester ME1 23 E1
Haig Villas ME3 8 C5
Hale Rd ME3 7 F2
Half Moon Way ME3 5 B3
Halifax Cl ME5 24 A4
Hall Rd ME5 29 F1
Halling By-Pass 6 C5
Hallsfield Rd ME5 28 B2
Hallwood Cl ME8 25 H5
Halstow La ME9 21 E5
Ham La ME7 29 H2
Ham River Hill ME3 7 E3
Hamelin Rd ME7 24 D2
Hamilton Ct ME5 24 B1
Hamilton Rd ME7 17 G1
Hamond Hill ME4 3 A2
Hampshire Cl ME5 24 B3
Hampton Cl ME5 23 H5
Hamwick Grn ME5 29 F3
Hancock Cl ME2 11 H4
Hannah Cl ME4 17 E5
Hanover Dr ME8 30 D1
Hanway ME8 18 B6
Harcourt Gdns ME8 26 A6
Hardinge Cl ME8 25 H6
Hards Town ME4 3 D3
Hardy Cl ME5 24 A4
Hare St ME4 17 E5
Harebell Cl ME5 23 F6
Haredale Cl ME1 23 E3
Harlech Cl ME2 11 F4
Harman Ct ME8 29 E2
Harold Av ME7 17 H3
Harold Rd ME2 14 C5
Harp Farm Rd ME5 29 G5
Harptree Dr ME5 23 F5
Harriet Dr ME1 15 G5
Harris Ct ME7 18 A6
Harrison Dr ME3 5 A1
Harrow Rd ME7 25 E4
Hartington St ME4 17 E5
Hartley Mews ME8 18 C4
Hartlip Hill ME9 27 G3
Hartpiece Cl ME8 19 G6
Harty Av ME8 30 D1
Harvel Av ME2 11 F6
Harvesters Cl ME8 26 A4
Harvey Rd ME8 26 D1
Harwood Rd ME8 26 D1
Hatfield Rd ME2 11 G5
Hathaway Ct ME1 3 A6
Hatton Rd ME5 29 G2
Haven Cl ME1 16 A6
Haven St ME3 7 F4
Haven Way ME4 13 F4
Havisham Cl ME1 16 A6
Hawbeck Rd ME8 31 E1
Hawkenbury Rise
  ME3 11 H3
Hawkhurst Rd ME8 18 C4
Hawkins Rd ME4 16 D2
Hawkwood Cl ME1 16 B3
Hawser Rd ME1 22 D1
Hawthorn Rd ME2 15 E2
Hawthorne Av ME8 18 D6
Hawthorns ME5 28 D3
Hayes Cl ME3 10 C2
Hayfields ME5 29 H3
Hayley Cl ME2 14 C5
Haymen St ME4 16 C5
Hayward Av ME2 11 H5
Hazel Gro ME5 24 A2
Hazlemere Dr ME7 18 B2
Headcorn Rd ME8 18 D4
Heather Cl ME5 23 G6
Heathfield Cl ME5 24 A3
Hellyar Ct ME1 16 A4
Hempstead Rd ME7 25 E5
Hempstead Valley Dr
  ME7 25 F4
Henley Cl,
  Chatham ME5 23 H4
Henley Cl,
  Gillingham ME8 26 A2
Henrietta Chase ME4 13 F3
Henry St,
  Chatham ME4 17 F5
Henry St,
  Gillingham ME8 26 C1
Hepplewhite Mews
  ME5 28 D4
Herbert Rd,
  Chatham ME4 17 E5
Herbert Rd,
  Gillingham ME8 26 A2
Herberts Ct ME3 5 C4
Herdsdown ME3 9 E4
Hereford Cl ME8 19 F6
Heritage Dr ME7 24 D1

Heritage Rd ME5 23
Herman Ter ME4 17
Hermitage Rd ME5 10
Herne Rd ME8 18
Hero Walk ME1 22
Heron Cl ME9 21
Heron Way,
  Chatham ME5 23
Heron Way,
  Rochester ME3 11
Hertsfield Av ME3 11
Herying Cl ME2 6
Hever Croft ME2 15
Hewitt Cl ME7 18
Hickory Dell ME7 25
Higgins La ME4 3
High Bank ME1 15
High Dewar Rd ME8 26
High Elms ME8 19
High St,
  Brompton ME7 17
High St,
  Chatham ME4 3
High St,
  Gillingham ME7 17
High St, Halling ME2 6
High St,
  Isle of Grain ME3 4
High St,
  Lower Stoke ME3 5
High St,
  Rainham ME8 26
High St,
  Rochester ME1 3
High St,
  Rochester ME1 3
High St, Strood ME2 11
High St, Upnor ME2 12
High Vw ME3 10
Higham Rd, Cliffe ME3 6
Higham Rd,
  Wainscott ME3 12
Highfield Cl ME8 25
Highfield Rd ME8 25
Highgrove Rd ME5 23
Highlands Cl ME2 14
Highridge ME7 24
Highview Dr ME5 23
Highwoods Cl ME3 10
Hilary Gdns ME1 15
Hilda Rd ME4 16
Hill Chase ME5 28
Hill Ct ME3 8
Hill Farm Cl ME3 5
Hill Rd,
  Rochester ME1 15
Hill Rd,
  Wouldham ME1 22
Hill View Cotts ME3 5
Hill View Way ME5 23
Hillborough Gro ME5 29
Hillcrest Dr ME2 14
Hillcrest Rd ME4 16
Hills Ter ME4 3
Hillshaw Cres ME2 14
Hillside ME1 15
Hillside Av ME2 11
Hillside Rd ME4 17
Hilltop Rd ME2 12
Hillyfield Cl ME2 11
Hilton Rd ME3 7
Hinton Cres ME7 25
Hoath Cl ME8 25
Hoath La ME8 25
Hoath Way ME8 25
Holborn La ME4 3
Holcombe Rd,
  Chatham ME4 16
Holcombe Rd,
  Rochester ME1 16
Holder Cl ME5 24
Holding St ME8 26
Holland Rd ME5 23
Hollingbourne Rd
  ME8 19
Hollow La ME9 27
Holly Cl,
  Chatham ME5 24
Holly Cl,
  Gillingham ME7 18
Holly Rd,
  Rochester ME2 15
Holly Rd,
  Wainscott ME3 12
Hollytree Dr ME3 10
Hollywood La ME3 11
Holmes Cl ME3 5
Holmoaks ME8 19
Holmside ME7 17

Meresborough La ME8 — 26 C5
Meresborough Rd ME8 — 26 C4
Mereworth Cl ME8 — 18 C4
Meridian Pk ME2 — 16 C1
Merivale Gro ME5 — 23 H6
Mermaid Cl ME4 — 23 H4
Merrals Wood Rd ME2 — 14 D3
Merryboys Rd ME3 — 7 E1
Merryfields ME2 — 11 G4
Merton Cl ME5 — 24 B6
Micawber Cl ME8 — 28 D4
Middle St ME7 — 17 E1
Middlefields ME8 — 26 C2
Middleton Cl ME8 — 26 A6
Mierscourt Cl ME8 — 26 C2
Mierscourt Rd ME8 — 26 B3
Milburn Rd ME7 — 17 G1
Miles Pl ME1 — 16 B4
Military Rd ME4 — 3 B2
Mill Cl ME2 — 11 H5
Mill Hill ME9 — 27 H2
Mill La, Blue Bell Hill ME5 — 28 B4
Mill La, Chatham ME5 — 24 B1
Mill La, Sittingbourne ME9 — 27 G4
Mill Rd, Gillingham ME7 — 17 F2
Mill Rd, Rochester ME2 — 11 H5
Millcroft Rd ME8 — 6 B2
Miller Way ME2 — 12 A3
Millfields ME5 — 29 H3
Millfordhope Rd ME2 — 10 C6
Millpond Cl ME2 — 11 G6
Mills Ter ME4 — 17 E5
Milner Rd ME7 — 17 H1
Milsted Rd ME8 — 18 D5
Milton Av ME3 — 7 E2
Milton Rd ME7 — 17 G4
Mincers Cl ME5 — 29 F3
Minerva Rd ME4 — 11 G5
Minor Canon Row ME1 — 3 B5
Minster Rd ME8 — 18 D5
Miskin Rd ME3 — 9 F4
Mitchell Av ME4 — 16 D6
Mitre Rd ME1 — 15 H4
Monarch St ME4 — 23 H4
Monkwood Cl ME1 — 22 C2
Monmouth Cl ME8 — 19 F6
Montford Rd ME5 — 28 C2
Montfort Rd ME2 — 11 G6
Montgomery Av ME5 — 23 H3
Montgomery Rd ME7 — 17 G4
Montrose Av ME5 — 17 H6
Moonstone Dr ME5 — 29 F2
Moor Park Cl ME8 — 26 C2
Moor St ME8 — 26 D2
Moore St ME5 — 11 G5
Mooring Rd ME1 — 23 E1
Morden St ME1 — 16 A4
Morement Rd ME3 — 9 F3
Morgan Cl ME8 — 26 A6
Morgan Rd ME2 — 11 G6
Morland Dr ME2 — 11 G5
Morning Cross Cotts ME3 — 6 C3
Mortimers Av ME3 — 7 E2
Mossbank ME5 — 29 E2
Mossy Glade ME8 — 26 A4
Motney Hill Rd ME8 — 19 H4
Mouat St ME5 — 29 E2
Mount La ME9 — 27 F6
Mount Pleasant ME5 — 17 E4
Mount Rd, Chatham ME4 — 16 D5
Mount Rd, Rochester ME1 — 15 G6
Mountbatten Av, Chatham ME5 — 23 H3
Mountbatten Av, Rochester ME3 — 10 C1
Moyle Cl ME8 — 26 A6
Mozart Ct ME4 — 16 C5
Mulberry Cl ME7 — 25 F6
Munns La ME9 — 27 G5
Murray Rd ME2 — 12 A5
Myrtle Cres ME5 — 23 G6

Nags Head La ME1 — 16 B3
Napier Rd ME7 — 17 H4
Napwood Cl ME8 — 25 H4
Nares Rd ME8 — 31 F1
Nash Cl ME5 — 29 F3

Nashenden Farm La ME1 — 22 A1
Nashenden La ME1 — 15 G6
Natal Rd ME4 — 16 D5
Naylors Cotts ME7 — 30 C4
Neale St ME4 — 16 D5
Nelson Ct ME5 — 24 B1
Nelson Rd ME7 — 17 G3
Nelson Ter ME5 — 24 B1
Neptune Bsns Est ME2 — 12 C6
Neptune Cl ME2 — 16 C1
Neptune Way ME2 — 16 C1
Neville Rd ME4 — 16 C6
New Covenant Pl ME1 — 16 B3
New Cut ME4 — 3 A2
New Rd, Chatham ME4 — 3 B3
New Rd, Cliffe ME3 — 6 B3
New Rd, Rochester ME1 — 16 B3
New Road Av ME4 — 3 A2
New St ME4 — 16 C4
New Stairs ME7 — 16 D2
Newark Ct*, North St ME2 — 11 H6
Newark Yd ME2 — 11 H6
Newbury St ME7 — 17 G3
Newenden Rd ME2 — 12 A4
Newington Ind Est ME9 — 27 H4
Newitt Rd ME3 — 9 F4
Newnham Cl ME8 — 19 E5
Newnham St ME4 — 17 E5
Newton Cl ME5 — 29 G3
Nicklaus Dr ME5 — 28 D2
Nickleby Cl ME1 — 16 A6
Nightingale Cl ME8 — 26 A4
Nile Rd ME7 — 17 G4
Nine Acres Rd ME8 — 14 B5
Niven Cl ME8 — 12 A2
Norah La ME3 — 10 B1
Nore Cl ME7 — 24 C1
Norfolk Cl, Chatham ME5 — 29 F2
Norfolk Cl, Gillingham ME8 — 19 E6
Norman Cl, Gillingham ME8 — 25 F6
Norman Cl, Rochester ME2 — 15 F3
Norreys Rd ME8 — 26 A3
North Bank Cl ME2 — 15 F3
North Dane Rd ME5 — 24 B4
North Rd, Gillingham ME7 — 17 E1
North Rd, Rochester ME3 — 6 B1
North Side Three Rd ME4 — 13 F5
North St ME2 — 11 H6
Northbourne Rd ME8 — 18 C4
Northcote Rd ME2 — 15 G1
Northgate ME1 — 3 B5
Northpoint Bsns Est ME2 — 12 B5
Northumberland Av ME8 — 26 B1
Northwood Av ME5 — 5 A1
Norton Gro ME5 — 28 C1
Norwich Ct ME5 — 14 D2
Norwood Cl ME3 — 6 B3
Nottingham Walk ME2 — 14 D2
Nursery Gdns ME3 — 9 G5
Nursery Rd ME8 — 25 H2
Nutfield Cl ME5 — 24 A2

Oak Av ME7 — 18 A2
Oak Dr ME3 — 10 C2
Oak La ME9 — 20 C6
Oak Rd ME2 — 15 E2
Oakhurst Cl ME8 — 28 D1
Oakland Cl ME5 — 28 D1
Oakleigh Cl ME5 — 28 C2
Oaks Bsns Village ME5 — 29 F4
Oaks Dene ME8 — 28 D4
Oakum Ct ME4 — 17 F6
Oastview ME8 — 26 C2
Ocelot Ct ME5 — 17 F5
Octavia Ct ME5 — 29 E1
Officers Rd ME4 — 13 E6
Officers Ter ME4 — 12 D6
Old Barn Cl ME7 — 25 E5
Old Castle Walk ME7 — 31 F1
Old Chatham Rd ME20 — 28 B6
Old George Ct ME3 — 8 B5

Old Guard Ho ME3 — 4 C6
Old House Rd ME9 — 27 G6
Old Pattens La ME1 — 16 B5
Old Rd ME4 — 3 B3
Old School Ct ME3 — 8 B5
Old Watling St ME4 — 10 B6
Oldcastle Walk ME8 — 26 A6
Oldfield Cl ME8 — 25 H2
Oliver Cl ME4 — 17 F6
Oliver Twist Cl ME1 — 15 H4
Olivier Dr ME3 — 11 H3
Olivine Cl ME5 — 29 E4
Olliffes Cl ME5 — 28 D3
Onslow Rd ME1 — 16 B5
Opal Grn ME5 — 29 E5
Orange Ter ME1 — 16 B3
Orbit Cl ME5 — 29 E5
Orchard Av ME2 — 11 F5
Orchard St ME8 — 26 A3
Orchard Villas ME4 — 3 C3
Orchid Cl ME7 — 14 C1
Ordnance St ME4 — 3 A3
Ordnance Ter ME4 — 3 A3
Orion Rd ME1 — 22 D3
Ormsby Grn ME8 — 31 F1
Osborne Rd ME7 — 17 G3
Osprey Av ME5 — 17 H6
Otterham Quay La ME8 — 26 D2
Otway St, Chatham ME4 — 17 E5
Otway St, Gillingham ME7 — 17 G2
Otway Ter ME4 — 17 E5
Owens Way ME7 — 18 B1
Oxford Rd ME7 — 17 H4

Packer Pl ME5 — 23 H3
Paget Row ME7 — 17 F3
Paget St ME7 — 17 F3
Pagitt St ME4 — 16 C6
Palace Ct ME5 — 17 H5
Palmers Ter ME5 — 5 C4
Palmerston Rd ME4 — 16 D6
Pankhurst Rd ME3 — 9 E3
Pannell Rd ME3 — 9 E3
Panton Cl ME5 — 29 F1
Papion Gro ME5 — 28 C3
Parham Rd ME4 — 16 D6
Park Av ME7 — 17 F3
Park Cres ME4 — 23 G2
Parker Cl ME8 — 26 A5
Parkfield Rd ME8 — 19 G6
Parkfields ME2 — 10 C6
Parkside ME7 — 7 E2
Parkwood Grn ME8 — 25 H5
Parr Av ME7 — 17 F3
Parsonage La ME2 — 12 A5
Partridge Dr ME4 — 13 E4
Partridge Rise ME4 — 13 F3
Pasley Rd ME7 — 17 E1
Pasley Rd East ME7 — 13 E6
Pasley Rd North ME7 — 13 E6
Pasley Rd West ME7 — 13 E6
Patrixbourne Av ME8 — 18 D6
Pattens Gdns ME1 — 16 B6
Pattens La ME4 — 16 B6
Pattens Pl ME1 — 16 B6
Patterns La ME1 — 23 E1
Payne Ct ME8 — 31 E1
Peacock Rise ME5 — 23 H6
Peal Cl ME8 — 9 G4
Pear Tree La ME7 — 24 C2
Pearman Ct ME8 — 26 C1
Peartree La ME1 — 10 A4
Peckham Cl ME2 — 12 A5
Peggoty Cl ME3 — 10 C2
Pelican Cl ME2 — 14 C1
Pemberton Sq ME2 — 12 A5
Pembroke Gdns ME8 — 26 A6
Pembroke Rd ME8 — 13 E6
Pembury Way ME8 — 19 F6
Penfold Cl ME5 — 23 H3
Penguin Cl ME2 — 14 D1
Pennant Rd ME1 — 22 D3
Penshurst Cl ME8 — 19 F6
Pentagon Shopping Centre ME4 — 3 B1
Pepys Way ME2 — 11 G4
Perie Row*, Westcourt St ME7 — 16 D1
Perry St ME4 — 16 C5
Peterborough Gdns ME2 — 14 D2
Petham Green ME8 — 18 D5
Peverel Grn ME8 — 31 E1
Phalarope Way ME4 — 13 G3
Pheasant Rd ME9 — 17 F6
Phillips Cl ME8 — 18 D6

Phoenix Ind Est ME2 — 12 A6
Phoenix Rd ME5 — 29 F3
Pickles Way ME3 — 6 A1
Pickwick Cres ME1 — 16 A5
Pier Approach Rd ME7 — 13 G6
Pier Pl ME2 — 12 D3
Pier Rd ME4,7 — 13 E5
Pier Rd Ind Est ME7 — 13 H6
Pikefields ME8 — 18 D5
Pilgrims Rd ME2 — 6 A4
Pilgrims Way ME2 — 14 C5
Pilot Rd ME1 — 22 D2
Pimpernel Way ME5 — 23 F6
Pine Gro ME7 — 25 E5
Pine Rd ME2 — 15 F2
Pinewood Dr ME8 — 29 H4
Pintail Cl ME3 — 4 C5
Pippin Croft ME7 — 25 F4
Pirbright St ME8 — 29 H3
Place La ME8 — 27 E5
Plantation Rd ME7 — 18 B2
Pleasant Row ME7 — 16 D1
Plomley Cl ME8 — 31 E1
Ploughman Way ME5 — 29 E4
Ploughmans Way ME8 — 26 A4
Plover Cl ME5 — 29 G3
Pluckley Cl ME8 — 18 D4
Plumtree Gro ME7 — 25 E6
Poachers Cl ME5 — 24 A5
Pochard Cl ME4 — 13 F4
Polhill Dr ME5 — 28 D3
Pond Hill ME3 — 6 B1
Poot La ME9 — 20 D3
Poplar Cl ME2 — 15 F3
Poplar Rd ME2 — 15 E3
Poplicans Rd ME2 — 14 B5
Poppy Cl ME7 — 18 A2
Port Cl ME5 — 29 F2
Port Rise ME4 — 16 D5
Port Victoria Rd ME3 — 4 D6
Portland Rd ME7 — 17 H2
Portland St ME4 — 17 E5
Portree Mews ME7 — 18 A5
Portsmouth Cl ME2 — 14 D2
Portway ME3 — 7 F2
Post Barn Rd ME4 — 16 D6
Pottery Rd ME3 — 9 F4
Povey Av ME3 — 12 A3
Power Station Rd ME8 — 12 A5
Powlett Rd ME2 — 24 D1
Preston Av ME7 — 24 D1
Preston Way ME8 — 18 D6
Pretoria Rd, Chatham ME4 — 16 D6
Pretoria Rd, Gillingham ME7 — 17 G4
Priestfield Rd ME7 — 17 H3
Priestfields ME1 — 15 H5
Primrose Av ME8 — 25 G6
Primrose Cl ME5 — 23 F3
Primrose Rd ME2 — 6 A5
Prince Arthur Rd ME7 — 17 E1
Prince Charles Av ME5 — 23 H6
Princes Av ME8 — 28 D1
Princes St ME1 — 16 A4
Princess Mary Av ME7 — 13 F6
Prinys Dr ME8 — 30 D1
Priory Ct ME8 — 18 B6
Priory Rd, Gillingham ME8 — 18 B5
Priory Rd, Rochester ME2 — 15 G1
Prospect Av ME2 — 11 H5
Prospect Pl ME1 — 15 G6
Prospect Row, Chatham ME4 — 16 D4
Prospect Row, Gillingham ME7 — 17 E2
Providence La ME1 — 3 C5
Pudding Rd ME8 — 26 C2
Puffin Rd ME3 — 4 C5
Pump La ME8 — 19 E6
Purbeck Rd ME4 — 16 C6
Purser Way ME7 — 13 G6
Pyrus Cl ME5 — 29 E4

Queen St, Chatham ME4 — 3 C2
Queen St, Rochester ME1 — 16 A4
Queendown Av ME8 — 25 H5
Queens Rd, Chatham ME5 — 17 G6

Queens Rd, Gillingham ME7 — 17
Queensway ME3 — 4
Queenswood Rd ME20 — 28
Quickrells Av ME3 — 6
Quickthorn Cres ME5 — 23
Quinion Cl ME5 — 28
Quinnell St ME8 — 26
Quixote Cres ME2 — 11

Radleigh Gdns ME1 — 23
Railway St, Chatham ME4 — 3
Railway St, Gillingham ME7 — 17
Rainham Rd ME5 — 17
Raleigh Cl ME5 — 23
Ramillies Cl ME5 — 23
Randall Rd ME4 — 23
Randolph Cotts ME7 — 11
Randolph Rd ME7 — 17
Ranscombe Cl ME2 — 14
Ratcliffe Highway, Allhallows ME3 — 4
Ratcliffe Highway, Hoo St Werburgh ME3 — 8
Ratcliffe Highway, Rochester ME3 — 5
Ravenswood Av ME2 — 11
Readscroft Rd ME8 — 25
Rectory Grange ME1 — 15
Redbridge Cl ME5 — 24
Rede Court Rd ME2 — 14
Redfern Av ME7 —
Redland Shaw ME1 — 23
Redshank Rd ME4 — 13
Redvers Rd ME4 — 16
Redwing Rd ME5 — 24
Redwood Cl ME5 — 29
Redwood Glade ME7 — 30
Reed St ME3 — 6
Reedham Cres ME3 — 7
Reform Rd ME4 — 17
Regency Cl ME4 — 30
Regent Rd ME7 —
Reginald Av ME2 — 14
Renown Rd ME5 — 29
Repton Way ME5 — 28
Resolution Cl ME5 — 23
Restharrow Way ME5 — 23
Restmore Cl ME3 — 6
Revenge Rd ME5 —
Reynolds Flds ME3 — 7
Rhode St ME4 — 3
Richard St, Chatham ME4 — 3
Richard St, Rochester ME1 — 16
Richborough Dr ME2 — 11
Richmond Cl, Chatham ME5 — 24
Richmond Cl, Rochester ME1 — 12
Richmond Rd ME7 — 17
Ridley Rd ME1 — 15
Riggal Cl ME2 — 14
Ringlet Rd ME4 — 13
Ringwood Cl ME8 — 26
Ripon Cl ME8 — 19
Rivendell Cl ME3 — 4
River Dr ME7 — 11
River St ME7 — 16
River Vw ME8 — 19
Rivermead ME4 — 13
Riverside Est ME2 — 16 C
Riverside One ME2 — 16 C
Riverside Three ME2 — 16 C
Riverside Two ME2 — 16 C
Roach St ME2 — 15 C
Roan Ct ME2 — 15
Roberts Rd ME8 — 26
Robin Hood La ME5 — 28
Robson Dr ME3 — 9
Robson Mews ME8 — 19
Rochester Av ME1 — 16
Rochester Bri ME1 — 3
Rochester Cl ME8 — 12
Rochester Cres ME3 — 9
Rochester Rd, Cuxton ME2 — 14
Rochester Rd, Rochester ME1 — 22
Rochester St ME4 — 3
Rock Av ME7 — 17 C
Rodkin Wood ME5 — 29

The Pinnacles ME4 13 F4
The Pintails ME4 13 F4
The Platters ME8 25 H3
The Poles ME9 20 D4
The Precinct ME1 3 B5
The Queen Mother Ct
ME1 15 H4
The Ridgeway,
Chatham ME4 23 F3
The Ridgeway,
Gillingham ME7 17 G1
The Rise,
Gillingham ME7 30 C2
The Rise,
Rochester ME1 16 B5
The Sally Port ME7 17 E2
The Shades ME2 10 C6
The Shoreway ME4 13 F3
The Spiers ME7 18 D2
The Spinney ME5 29 E3
The Spires ME2 14 D2
The Street,
Gillingham ME7 30 C4
The Street,
Hartlip ME9 27 F6
The Street,
High Halstow ME3 5 A2
The Street,
Lower Halstow ME9 21 G5
The Street, Stoke ME3 5 A6
The Street,
Upchurch ME9 20 D4
The Street,
Upper Hallng ME2 6 A5
The Terrace,
Chatham ME4 13 E6
The Terrace,
Rochester ME1 3 C6
The Tideway ME1 22 C3
The Vineries ME7 18 A2
The Wheelers ME8 25 G4
The Whimbrels ME4 13 F4
The Willows ME8 19 F6
The Wirrals ME5 28 D1
The Yard ME5 29 F2
Theodore Pl ME7 17 G2
Third Av,
Chatham ME5 24 A1
Third Av,
Gillingham ME7 18 A4
Thirlmere Cl,
Gillingham ME7 18 B2
Thirlmere Cl,
Rochester ME2 12 A4
Thistlebank ME5 29 E2
Thistledown Cl ME7 30 C1
Thomas St ME1 16 A4
Thompson Cl ME8 26 C2
Thorn Cl ME5 28 B4
Thorndale Cl ME5 23 E6
Thorndyke Cl ME4 23 G2
Thornham Rd ME8 19 E5
Thorold Rd ME5 17 F4
Thorpe Walk ME8 31 E2
Thrale Way ME8 26 A6
Thrush Cl ME5 24 A4
Thurston Dr ME2 11 E6
Tilbury Rd ME8 19 H6
Tilley Cl ME3 9 F5
Timber Bank ME5 23 H4
Timber Tops ME5 29 H4
Tintagel Cl ME2 15 G1
Tintagel Gds ME2 15 F1
Tobruk Way ME5 23 G4
Toddington Cres
ME5 28 B3
Toledo Pad ME7 17 H3
Tolgate La ME2 11 H6
Topley Dr ME3 5 B2
Toronto Rd ME7 18 A4
Tower Hill ME2 12 D3
Town Rd ME3 7 E4
Trafalgar St ME7 17 G3
Tramways ME5 17 G6
Transon Ho*,
The Fairway ME1 22 D1
Travertine Rd ME5 29 E4
Trelawn Cres ME5 29 F2
Trent Rd ME5 24 A5
Trevale Rd ME1 22 C1
Trevino Dr ME5 28 D2
Trident Cl ME2 16 B1

Trinity Rd ME7 17 F1
Trotwood Cl ME5 29 E4
Trubridge Rd ME3 9 F4
Truro Cl ME8 19 E5
Tudor Gro,
Gillingham ME8 26 B2
Tudor Gro,
Rochester ME3 8 B5
Tufa Cl ME5 29 F4
Tufton Rd ME8 26 B1
Tunbury Av ME5 28 D2
Tunbury Av South
ME5 28 D3
Tupman Cl ME7 15 H4
Turner St ME3 6 B2
Turnstone Rd ME5 29 G3
Tuscan Dr ME5 29 F4
Two Posts Alley ME1 3 B4
Twogates Hill ME3 7 C4
Twydall Grn ME8 18 D5
Twydall La ME8 18 C6
Twyford ME8 19 H6
Tyler Dr ME8 31 F1
Tyne Cl ME5 24 A5

Underdown Av ME4 23 G1
Union St,
Chatham ME4 3 D3
Union St,
Rochester ME1 16 A3
Upbury Way ME4 3 D3
Upchat Rd ME3 8 A5
Uplands Cl ME2 14 D2
Upnor Rd ME2 12 B4
Upper Britton Pl ME7 17 F3
Upper East Rd ME4 13 F6
Upper Luton Rd ME5 17 F5
Upper Robin Hood La
ME5 28 B3
Urquhart Cl ME5 23 H6

Vale Dr ME5 23 E5
Valentine Cl ME8 25 E1
Valentine Dr ME5 5 B2
Valerian Cl ME5 28 C1
Valetta Way ME1 15 H3
Valiant Rd ME5 29 F3
Valley Rd ME7 18 A3
Valley Rise ME5 28 D3
Valley View Rd ME1 22 C1
Vancouver Dr ME8 25 H1
Vange Mews ME1 15 H3
Vanguard Way ME2 12 B5
Ventnor Cl ME5 24 A2
Vicarage Cl,
Halling ME2 6 C5
Vicarage Cl,
Stoke ME3 5 A6
Vicarage La,
Hoo St Werburgh
ME3 9 G5
Vicarage La,
Sittingbourne ME9 21 G5
Vicarage La,
Stoke ME3 5 A6
Vicarage Rd,
Gillingham ME7 17 F3
Vicarage Rd,
Halling ME2 6 A5
Vicarage Rd,
Strood ME2 11 H6
Vicarage Row ME3 10 C1
Victoria Rd,
Chatham ME4 17 F6
Victoria Rd,
Walderslade ME5 28 C2
Victoria St,
Gillingham ME7 17 G2
Victoria St,
Rochester ME1 3 C6
Victoria St,
Strood ME2 11 H6
Victoria Ter ME1 15 G6
Victory
Bsns Pk ME2 12 B6
Vidgeon Av ME3 9 E3
View Rd ME3 7 E2
Viewlands ME5 17 F5
Viking Cl ME2 15 F3
Villa Rd ME3 10 B2
Village Vw ME5 17 G6
Vincent Rd ME20 28 A6

Vines La ME1 3 B6
Vineyard Cres ME8 26 D1
Violet Cl ME5 29 E5
Virginia Rd ME7 13 G6
Vixen Cl ME5 24 A4
Vulcan Cl ME5 24 A3

Wadlands Rd ME3 6 B2
Waghorn St ME4 17 E5
Wainscott Rd ME2 12 B4
Wainscott Walk ME2 12 B3
Wake Rd ME1 22 D2
Wakefield Cl ME2 14 D2
Wakeley Rd ME8 26 C1
Walderslade Rd
ME4,5 23 F2
Walderslade Woods
ME5 28 B2
Waleys Cl ME8 26 D1
Wall Cl ME3 9 E3
Wallace Rd ME1 23 E2
Wallbridge La ME8 20 C5
Walmers Av ME3 10 B2
Walnut Cl ME5 24 A3
Walsham Rd ME5 28 C4
Walsingham Cl ME8 31 E2
Walters Rd ME3 9 F3
Waltham Rd ME8 18 D5
Warblers Cl ME2 11 G6
Warden Rd ME1 16 A5
Wardwell La ME9 21 G5
Warlingham Cl ME8 20 A6
Warlingham Rd ME8 26 D1
Warner St ME4 16 D5
Warren Rd ME5 28 B4
Warren Wood Rd
ME1 22 D3
Warwick Cres ME1 15 F6
Watchmans Ter ME5 17 G6
Water Works La ME8 25 G1
Waterloo Rd ME7 17 G3
Watermeadow Cl
ME7 24 D4
Watermill Cl ME2 12 A5
Waters Pl ME7 25 E4
Waterside Cl ME2 16 C1
Waterside La ME7 18 B1
Watling Av ME5 17 H6
Watling St,
Gillingham ME7 17 H5
Watling St,
Rochester ME2 10 C6
Watson Av ME5 23 E6
Watts Av ME1 16 A3
Watts St ME4 16 D5
Waverley Cl ME5 29 H3
Wayfield Rd ME5 23 G4
Wayweed Av ME5 28 C1
Wealden Ct ME5 17 F5
Weatherly Cl ME1 16 A4
Weavering Cl ME2 11 H3
Webb Cl ME3 9 F3
Webster Rd ME8 26 B1
Wedgewood Dr ME5 23 H3
Weeds Wood Rd
ME5 23 G6
Well Penn Rd ME3 6 C3
Weller Av ME1 16 B6
Wellington Rd ME7 17 G4
Wells Ct ME2 14 D3
Wells Rd ME2 14 D3
Wemmick Cl ME1 23 E3
Wendover Cl ME2 6 D5
Wentworth Dr,
Gillingham ME8 26 A4
Wentworth Dr,
Rochester ME3 7 F1
West Dr ME5 23 E5
West La ME3 4 B4
West Motney Way
ME8 19 H4
West St, Cliffe ME3 6 A1
West St,
Gillingham ME7 17 G2
West St,
Rochester ME2 11 H4
Westbrooke Cl ME4 17 E6
Westcourt St ME7 16 D1
Westergate Rd ME2 11 F5
Westerham Cl ME8 18 D4
Western Av ME4 13 D3

Westfield
Bsns Centre ME2 12 A6
Westfield Cotts ME9 21 F6
Westfield Sole Rd
ME14 29 G5
Westgate ME4 13 E3
Westmoreland Dr
ME9 21 G5
Westmount Av ME4 3 B3
Weston Rd ME2 11 G6
Westview ME4 13 F3
Wetheral Dr ME5 24 A6
Wey Cl ME5 24 A5
Wharf La ME3 6 C1
Wharf Rd ME7 13 G6
Wheatcroft Gro ME8 26 B3
Wheatear Way ME5 24 A4
Wheatfields ME5 29 H3
Whiffens Av ME4 3 C1
Whiffens Av West
ME4 3 C1
Whimbrel Walk ME5 29 G3
Whitcombe Cl ME5 29 F2
White Hill Rd ME14 31 E3
White Leaves Rise
ME2 14 C5
White Rd ME4 23 G1
Whitegate Ct ME5 26 A5
Whitehorse Hill ME5 17 F5
Whitehouse Cl ME3 9 G5
Whitewall Rd ME2 12 B6
Whitewall Way ME2 12 B6
Whittaker St ME4 3 C3
Whyman Av ME4 23 G1
Wickham St ME1 16 B5
Widgeon Rd ME2 14 D2
Wigmore Rd ME8 25 F5
Wildfell Cl ME5 29 F5
Wildman Cl ME8 31 E2
Wildwood Glade ME7 25 F6
Wilks Cl ME8 20 A6
Will Adams Way ME8 25 E1
William Rd ME2 14 C5
William St ME8 26 C1
Willow Grange ME8 9 F5
Willow Rd ME2 15 F2
Willowbank Dr ME3 5 B3
Willowby Gdns ME8 31 G1
Willowherb Cl ME4 13 E4
Wilmington Way ME8 18 C6
Wilson Av ME1 23 E1
Wiltshire Cl ME5 24 B2
Wimbourne Dr ME8 26 A4
Winchelsea Rd ME5 24 A5
Winchester Av ME5 28 D1
Winchester Way ME8 26 C2
Windermere Dr ME8 25 H4
Windmill Ct ME2 11 H4
Windmill Cotts ME5 5 C4
Windmill Rd ME7 17 F5
Windmill St ME2 11 H4
Windsor Av ME4 16 D6
Windsor Ct ME7 17 H2
Windsor Rd ME7 17 H2
Windward Rd ME1 22 D1
Windyridge ME7 24 D1
Winford Mews ME1 15 G6
Wingham Cl ME8 18 D5
Wingrove Dr ME2 12 A6
Winston Dr ME2 12 B3
Winston Rd ME2 14 D2
Wintergreen Cl ME4 13 F4
Witham Way ME2 15 F1
Wittersham Cl ME5 24 A5
Wiverhoe Cl ME8 19 H6
Wollaston Cl ME8 31 E2
Wood St,
Gillingham ME7 17 E1
Wood St,
Rochester ME2 11 H4
Woodbury Rd ME5 28 C4
Woodchurch Cl ME5 24 A5
Woodchurch Cres
ME8 18 D6
Woodfield Way ME3 12 B1
Woodhurst ME5 28 B1
Woodhurst Cl ME4 14 C6
Woodlands ME5 29 E3
Woodlands Ct ME5 23 F2
Woodlands Rd ME7 18 A6
Woodlark Rd ME4 13 E4

Woodpecker Glade
ME8 25
Woodruff Cl ME8 20
Woodrush Pl ME4 13
Woodside ME8 25
Woodside Grn ME3 7
Woodstock Rd ME4 15
Woodview Rise ME2 11
Woolbrook Cl ME8 20
Wooldeys Rd ME8 19
Woolwich Cl ME5 23
Wootton Grn ME8 19
Wopsle Cl ME1 23
Worcester Cl ME2 11
Wordsworth Cl ME5 24
Wouldham Rd ME1 15
Wren Way ME5 24
Wright Cl ME8 18
Wulfere Way ME2 12
Wyatt Pl ME2 15
Wykeham St ME2 11
Wyles Rd ME4 16
Wyles St ME7 17
Wylie Rd ME3 9
Wyndham Rd ME4 16
Wyvill Cl ME8 16

Yalding Cl ME2 11
Yantlet Dr ME2 10
Yarrow Rd ME5 23
Yaugher La ME9 27
Yelsted La,
Maidstone ME14 29
Yelsted La,
Sittingbourne ME9 31
Yelsted Rd ME9 31
Yeoman Dr ME7 24
Yew Tree Cl ME8 25
Yokosuka Way ME7 18
York Av,
Chatham ME5 28
York Av,
Gillingham ME7 17
York Hill ME5 17
York Rd ME1 16

Zetland Av ME7 18
Zillah Gdns ME8 25

Red Books *showing the way*

r the latest publication list, prices and to order online please visit our website.

CAL STREET ATLASES

ngdon, Didcot
ershot, Camberley
eton, Belper
lover
ford, Tenterden
esbury, Tring
gor, Caernarfon
astaple, Bideford
Jdon, Billericay
ngstoke, Alton
, Bradford-on-Avon
ford
min, Wadebridge
memouth
cknell
ntwood
hton
tol
mley
ton upon Trent
w Saint Edmunds, Stowmarket
bridge
nock, Rugeley
diff
isle, Penrith
lmsford, Braintree
ster, Wrexham
sterfield, Dronfield
chester, Bognor Regis
openham, Calne
tbridge, Airdrie
chester, Clacton-on-Sea
oy, Kettering, Wellingborough
entry, Rugby
wley, Mid-Sussex
we, Nantwich
by
adee, Saint Andrews
tbourne, Hailsham
nburgh
ter, Exmouth
rk, Grangemouth
eham, Gosport
shire Towns
kestone, Dover
sgow
ucester, Cheltenham
vesend, Dartford
ys, Thurrock
at Yarmouth, Lowestoft
insby, Cleethorpes
ildford, Woking
milton, Motherwell
low, Bishops Stortford
rogate, Knaresborough
stings, Bexhill
eford
tford, Waltham Cross
h Wycombe
itingdon, Saint Neots
wich

Isle of Man
Isle of Wight
Kendal, Windermere
Kidderminster, Stourport-on-Severn
Kingston upon Hull
Lancaster, Morecambe
Leicester
Lincoln, Washingborough
Llandudno, Colwyn Bay
Loughborough, Coalville
Luton, Dunstable
Macclesfield, Wilmslow
Maidstone
Mansfield, Sutton in Ashfield
Medway, Gillingham
Mid Wales Towns
Milton Keynes
New Forest
Newark-on-Trent
Newbury, Thatcham
Newport, Chepstow
Newquay, Perranporth
Northampton
Northwich, Winsford
Norwich
Nottingham
Nuneaton, Bedworth
Oxford, Kidlington
Penzance, Saint Ives
Perth, Kinross
Peterborough, Stamford
Plymouth
Portsmouth
Reading, Henley-on-Thames
Redditch, Kidderminster
Reigate, Mole Valley
Rhyl, Prestatyn
Rugby
Saint Albans, Welwyn, Hatfield
Saint Austell, Lostwithiel
Salisbury, Wilton
Scarborough, Whitby
Scunthorpe
Sevenoaks
Shrewsbury
Sittingbourne, Faversham
Slough, Maidenhead, Windsor
Solihull
Southampton
Southend-on-Sea
Stafford
Stevenage, Letchworth
Stirling, Alloa
Stoke-on-Trent
Stroud, Nailsworth
Swansea
Swindon, Chippenham
Tamworth, Lichfield
Taunton, Bridgwater
Shrewsbury, Telford
Tenby, Saundersfoot
Thanet, Canterbury

Torbay, Newton Abbot
Trowbridge, Frome
Truro, Falmouth
Tunbridge Wells, Tonbridge
Walsall
Warwick, Royal Leamington Spa
Watford, Hemel Hempstead
Wells, Glastonbury
West Midlands, Birmingham
Weston-super-Mare
Weymouth, Dorchester
Winchester
Worcester
Wolverhampton (Folded Map)
Workington, Whitehaven
Worthing, Littlehampton
Wrexham
York

COUNTY STREET ATLASES
(Town Centre Maps)
Bedfordshire
Berkshire
Buckinghamshire
Cambridgeshire
Cheshire
Cornwall
Cumbria
Derbyshire
Devon
Dorset
East Sussex
Essex
Gloucestershire
Hampshire
Herefordshire
Hertfordshire
Kent
Leicestershire, Rutland
Lincolnshire
Norfolk
Northamptonshire
Nottinghamshire
Oxfordshire
Shropshire
Somerset
Staffordshire
Suffolk
Surrey
Warwickshire
West Sussex
Wiltshire
Worcestershire

EUROPEAN STREET MAPS
Calais & Boulogne Shoppers Map (Folded Map)
Dieppe Shoppers Map (Folded Map)
North French Towns Street Atlas

RED BOOKS (ESTATE PUBLICATIONS) Ltd, Bridewell House, Tenterden, Kent. TN30 6EP
Tel: 01580 764225   Fax: 01580 763720   Email: sales@redbooks-maps.co.uk

Red Books *showing the way*

For the latest publication list, prices and to order online please visit our websit

LEISURE & TOURIST MAPS

MOTORING ATLASES

Britain (290x400mm) (Paperback or Wiro)
Britain & Ireland Compact (A5) (Wiro)

EUROPEAN LEISURE MAPS

Belgium, Luxembourg & Netherlands
Cross Channel Visitors Map
Europe
France & Belgium
Germany
Ireland
Italy
Spain & Portugal

WORLD MAPS

Political (Folded or Flat in Tube)
Travel Adventure Map (Folded or Flat in Tube)

RED BOOKS (ESTATE PUBLICATIONS) Ltd, Bridewell House, Tenterden, Kent. TN30 6EP
Tel: 01580 764225   Fax: 01580 763720   Email: sales@redbooks-maps.co.uk